Get Started

Baking

Get Started

Baking

LONDON, NEW YORK, MUNICH, MELBOURNE, DELHI

Senior Editor Alastair Laing
Project Art Editor Gemma Fletcher
Managing Editor Penny Warren
Managing Art Editor Alison Donovan
Senior Jacket Creative Nicola Powling
Jacket Design Assistant Rosie Levine
Pre-production Producer Sarah Isle
Producer Jen Lockwood
Art Directors Peter Luff, Jane Bull
Publisher Mary Ling

DK Publishing
North American Consultant Kate Curnes
Editor Margaret Parrish
Senior Editor Rebecca Warren

DK India
Senior Editor Garima Sharma
Senior Art Editor Ivy Roy
Managing Editor Alka Thakur Hazarika
Deputy Managing Art Editor Priyabrata Roy Chowdhury

Tall Tree Ltd.
Editor Emma Marriott
Designer Ben Ruocco

Written by Amanda Wright

First American Edition, 2013

Published in the United States by DK Publishing,
375 Hudson Street, New York, New York 10014

13 14 15 16 17 10 9 8 7 6 5 4 3 2 1
001—187845—Jan/2013

Published in Great Britain by Dorling Kindersley Limited.

A catalog record for this book is available from the
Library of Congress.

ISBN 978-1-4654-0195-3

DK books are available at special discounts when purchased
in bulk for sales promotions, premiums, fund-raising, or
educational use. For details, contact: DK Publishing Special
Markets, 375 Hudson Street, New York, New York 10014
or SpecialSales@dk.com.

Printed and bound by Leo Paper Products Ltd., China

Discover more at
www.dk.com

Contents

1
Start Simple

2
Build On It

3
Take It Further

PUBLISHER'S NOTE
The recipes contained in this book have
been created for the ingredients and
techniques indicated. The Publisher is
not responsible for your specific health
or allergy needs that may require
supervision. Nor is the Publisher
responsible for any adverse reactions
you may have to the recipes contained
in the book, whether you follow them
as written or modify them to suit your
personal dietary needs or tastes.

Build Your Course

This book is divided into broad sections that allow you to build a three-stage course in baking. All areas are covered, from quick cakes to artisan breads, with recipes that increase in difficulty to develop your skill set and offer new challenges as you grow in confidence and experience.

From novice to master baker

Take your first steps with the recipes in Start Simple, which are easy to master and provide essential foundation skills. In Build On It you will discover many classic baked goods and, once they are added to your repertoire, you can call yourself a skilled baker. The recipes in the Take It Further section have the "wow!" factor to stretch you and give you a chance to show off.

Recipe information

Symbols highlight the number of servings from each recipe, how long it takes to bake, and whether it can be frozen.

These details feature at the start of each recipe

Makes 18

Bakes in 10–15 minutes

Up to 8 weeks

Tip Boxes Crucial pieces of advice are highlighted in pullout boxes that will help you to achieve the best possible results.

Clear photography demonstrates how to perform each technique correctly

"How to" **Pages**

Each area of baking is introduced on "How to" pages, which pinpoint the key techniques to understand before you tackle a recipe. Here you learn not only the "how?" but also the "why?"—since understanding the reasons for doing something is crucial to getting it right.

1 After learning about the key techniques, you then put these into practice with an illustrated step-by-step recipe. A visual checklist of ingredients and special equipment, plus a detailed timeline, are included to help you plan.

Useful Advice Recipes are full of tips, reminders, warnings, and advice about what to do if things go wrong—its' like having your own tutor help out in the kitchen.

Annotations highlight what to do and how things should look at key stages ......

Achieving **Perfect Results**

At the end of each illustrated practice recipe, a realistic image of the finished baked good demonstrates the results you should be aiming for.

Photographs show the right color, texture, and decorative presentation you should try to match ...

Qualities to strive for with each recipe are identified with annotations

Room for improvement?

Perfection can be difficult to achieve on the first attempt and below the image you will find common problems anticipated, explanations for

what probably went wrong, and advice for how to avoid making the same mistake next time.

Having mastered the practice recipe over the page you will find further similar recipes to enjoy.

Now turn the page and start baking! ▶ ▶ ▶

Essential **Equipment**

MEASURING EQUIPMENT

Baking is a precise business and it's important to weigh and measure ingredients accurately. Scales are the most precise way to measure. Liquid and dry measuring cups are essential for baking, as are measuring spoons. Use either imperial (oz) or metric (g), but don't mix the two.

Scales
Accurate scales that weigh in small units are handy.

Liquid measuring cup
For liquids. Cups should measure both imperial and metric.

Dry measuring cups
Recipes measure by fractions of a cup.

Measuring spoons
For small quantities, from 1 tablespoon to ⅛ teaspoon.

MIXING EQUIPMENT

Basic mixing equipment should include different-sized mixing bowls and tools to sift, whisk, beat, combine, and fold in your ingredients.

Sieve
Sifting fine dry ingredients leaves them aerated and lump-free.

Wooden spoons
Strong and heat-resistant. For stirring, mixing, and creaming.

Large metal spoon
Bigger than a tablespoon. For folding in dry ingredients into cake mixtures.

Glass bowls
A selection of heavy-bottomed, wide-brimmed bowls is invaluable for mixing, beating, and folding.

Hand whisk and electric mixer
A handheld electric mixer is essential—since it makes light work of any cake mix—as is a handheld whisk, used for whisking egg whites, cream, and sauces.

Plastic spatula
Good for scraping out bowls, and leveling and spreading mixtures.

PASTRY EQUIPMENT

Pastry-making requires some simple but vital tools for rolling and cutting dough into shapes, brushing on glazes or greasing pans, and baking pie dough blind.

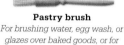

Pastry brush
For brushing water, egg wash, or glazes over baked goods, or for greasing pans or sheets.

Rolling pin
Essential for pastries, cookies, and Danish pastries. Choose a heavy wooden rolling pin with handles for best results.

Baking beans
Used to fill a pie crust when baking it blind before adding the filling.

Cookie cutters
A basic selection should include round and fluted cutters, as well as individually shaped cutters.

PANS AND SHEETS

A good selection of pans and sheets are essential in baking. Always use the correct-sized pan and buy pans that are strong and sturdy.

Loaf pan
Ideal for bread as well as loaf-shaped cakes, and available in various sizes.

Baking sheets
Various-sized baking sheets and pans will accommodate the different recipes you may want to make.

Tart pan
Tart pans with removable bottoms are essential for making sweet and savory tarts and pies.

Round cake pans
Available in many sizes, pans with removable bottoms are perfect for cakes, and springform versions, which open at the side, are more suited to cheesecakes or delicate sponge cakes.

Square cake pan
Perfect for cakes and brownies, square pans have a fixed bottom.

Cupcake or muffin pan
A 12-hole pan for cupcakes or muffins. Muffin pans have deeper molds.

ESSENTIAL EXTRAS

Metal skewer
A thin metal skewer is an essential tool for checking that your cakes are cooked properly.

Wire rack
Keep at least one wire rack, ideally a large one, on which your bakes and cakes can cool.

Palette knife
A long, flexible blade with a round end, useful for smoothing surfaces and easing pastry from pans.

Piping bag
A nylon piping bag with one plain and one star nozzle makes for perfect, basic piping equipment.

Parchment paper
For lining pans so the mix doesn't stick during baking, and to cover cakes if browning too much in the oven. Wax paper is very similar and a good alternative.

Essential **Ingredients**

FLOUR

Flour is the key ingredient in most baking recipes. There are different types of flour, each containing leavening agent. Most baking recipes will require one or a mix of these flours.

Cornstarch
A very fine flour made from the starch of corn kernels, typically used in shortbread for a light texture.

All-purpose flour
Contains 75% of the wheat grain and is used for many baking recipes, such as cakes, cookies, and pastries.

Self-rising flour
Contains 75% of the wheat grain and an added baking agent to aid consistent rising in cakes.

Bread flour
Made from durum wheat, with a higher protein and gluten content, making it perfect for bread.

Whole-wheat bread flour
A nuttier flour made from milling the whole grain. Perfect for bread-making.

SUGAR

Sugar sweetens baked goods, but also adds moisture, color, volume, and texture. It is available in different colors, from white to dark brown, and in varying granule size, from coarse to very fine. The type of recipe you make will dictate which type of sugar is best suited to it.

Brown sugar
This moist, soft grain sugar is perfect for adding more flavor to cakes.

Dark brown sugar
A strongly flavored, dark sugar that is perfect for fruit cakes.

Granulated sugar
Widely used in baking, since its very fine crystals make it easy to mix in and dissolve.

Golden caster sugar
Very fine crystals with molasses left in for color, this type of sugar is popular in the UK.

Sanding sugar
Medium-sized sugar crystals work best for jam-making and decoration of cookies and cakes.

Confectioners' sugar
A fine white powdered sugar, made from grinding granulated sugar, and mostly used for icings and decoration.

DAIRY

Most baking recipes require fat, usually in the form of butter, to add essential flavor, volume, and a light texture. Other dairy products are also frequently used for different purposes, such as adding richness and moisture to a cake mix, for a smooth filling, or whipped up as decoration.

Butter
Available in unsalted and salted varieties, butter comes in block form and works best at room temperature for cakes and chilled for pastry.

Heavy cream
Adds richness and moistness, and is ideal for whipping to fill and decorate desserts.

Buttermilk
Often used with baking soda, since the combination of the two acts as a leavening agent.

Plain yogurt
Adds moistness and also richness to baked recipes.

Mascarpone
A rich, silky-smooth Italian soft cream cheese, often used as an alternative to cream cheese.

Cream cheese
A soft, smooth cheese made with cream, most commonly used in cheesecakes.

ESSENTIAL EXTRAS

Eggs
Eggs add structure, moistness, flavor, and tenderness to baked goods and, unless otherwise specified, all recipes use large eggs.

LEAVENING AGENTS

Leavening agents ensure that cakes and cookies rise during baking by producing carbon dioxide bubbles when combined with heat, moisture, or acidity. These three leavening agents are the most commonly used and are widely available.

Chocolate
Used as chocolate chunks or cocoa powder; the higher the percentage of cocoa solids, the stronger the flavor.

Baking powder
Produces carbon dioxide when combined with heat and warmth and is widely used in baking.

Baking soda
Produces carbon dioxide when combined with moisture and acidic products, such as buttermilk, molasses, or lemon juice.

Dried yeast
Most commonly used in bread, and needs careful preparation with heat and moisture to work properly.

Gelatin
A translucent, tasteless substance made from animal by-products. Used for setting fillings and jellies, it is available in leaf or powder form.

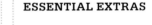

1

Start Simple

It is time to put on your apron and get cooking with a selection of simple, step-by-step recipes and techniques to get you started in the world of baking. Learn how to make quick batter-style cakes and breads, light-as-air meringues, simple cookies using the rubbed in and creaming methods, as well as creamy, crumbly cheesecakes and a first foray into pastry.

In this section, learn to bake:

Quick Cakes
pp.14–27

Cookies
pp.28–35

Cut-out Cookies
pp.36–43

Meringue
pp.44–55

No-bake Cheesecake
pp.56–63

Store-bought Pastry
pp.64–71

Quick Breads
pp.72–79

How to make **Quick Cakes**

Quick cakes are the simplest cakes to make, since many of the processes used in traditional cake-making are left out: you simply mix to form a batter. Depending on the ingredients, there are various ways of making the batter. The easiest is the "all-in-one" method where everything is simply mixed together all at once. Common to all is the need to combine wet and dry ingredients carefully for a smooth batter with good volume.

Gently tap the edge of the sieve against your hand to help with the sifting process

Hold the seive up as high as you dare to maximize contact with the air

Tip If you have time, sift the dry ingredients twice for a smoother, lighter mix.

Use a mixing bowl wider than the sieve to catch the flour

Sifting

Sift all your dry ingredients together through a sieve, holding the sieve high above the bowl. Sifting ingredients together mixes them, removes any lumps, and aerates the flour particles, which allows them to absorb liquids better and adds volume to the mix.

Pour the liquid into the well, then gradually draw the dry ingredients into the liquid

Create a well by drawing the dry ingredients out to the edges with your fingers or by using a wooden spoon

Mixing dry and wet ingredients

After beating the wet ingredients until properly mixed, make a well in the center of the flour mixture and pour in the liquid. A well helps to draw the dry ingredients into the wet ingredients a little at a time, so that you end up with a lump-free mixture. Alternatively, you can sift the dry ingredients into the wet ingredients and mix together.

Scrape down the sides of the bowl

To keep the air in the mix, stir the batter gently, using a figure-eight motion

Use a large spatula or metal spoon for easy mixing

Making the batter

Using a spatula, gently mix the wet and dry ingredients together until no flecks of flour are visible. Do not overbeat the mixture, since this will cause the gluten in the flour to develop too much and your cakes will end up on the heavy side.

Carrot Cake

This classic carrot cake is the ideal recipe to begin with.
Sift into your batter the dry ingredients and an array of
aromatic spices to make a deliciously moist and fruity
cake, topped with a silky-smooth cream cheese frosting.

Serves 8–10	Bakes in 45 minutes	Up to 8 weeks, unfrosted

ngredients

or the cake

cup sunflower oil, plus extra for greasing

large eggs

¼ cups light brown sugar

tsp pure vanilla extract

cups packed, peeled, coarsely grated carrots (about 3 small carrots)

cup (4oz) walnuts

cup golden raisins

½ cups self-rising flour

cup whole-wheat flour

tsp salt

1 tsp cinnamon

1 tsp ground ginger

¼ tsp finely grated nutmeg

finely grated zest of 1 orange

For the frosting

4 tbsp unsalted butter, softened

½ cup cream cheese, at room temperature

1½ cups confectioners' sugar

½ tsp vanilla extract

2 oranges

Special Equipment

9in (23cm) round springform cake pan

sunflower oil

eggs

brown sugar

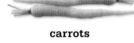

self-rising and whole-wheat flour   **carrots**   **vanilla extract**   **walnuts**   **golden raisins**

alt and spices   **unsalted butter**   **cream cheese**   **confectioners' sugar**   **oranges**   **springform cake pan**

Total time *1 hour 15 minutes, plus cooling*

Prepare	**Make**	**Bake**	**Decorate**
10 minutes	*10 minutes*	*45 minutes*	*10 minutes*

1 Preheat the oven to 350°F (180°C). Pour the oil and eggs into a large bowl along with the sugar and vanilla extract. Using a hand mixer, beat together until the mixture is slightly thickened.

Remember Make sure your ingredients are thoroughly mixed and smooth, otherwise you will have a lumpy cake.

Beat until the sugar has dissolved and the mixture has thickened enough to drop heavily from the beaters

2 Finely grate the carrots, then place them in a clean dish towel, or you can use a piece of muslin. Tighten the dish towel around the grated carrot and squeeze tightly to remove excess liquid. Discard the liquid.

Why? You drain the liquid from the carrots so that the batter does not become too wet and the cake bakes properly.

3 Fold the carrot into the batter until well mixed. Scatter the walnuts on a baking sheet and bake for 5 minutes in the preheated oven. Rub off their excess skin in a dish towel (see p.38). Coarsely chop and stir the walnuts into the batter along with the golden raisins.

Tip You don't have to bake the walnuts, but it helps when rubbing off their skins and enhances their flavor.

Do not overmix the cake batter or you will end up with a heavy cake

4 Sift the self-rising and whole-wheat flours together with the salt, cinnamon, ginger, and nutmeg, adding any bran left in the sieve. Stir in the orange zest and mix until all ingredients are incorporated and no flecks of flour are visible.

Tip Make sure you sift the flour from a decent height in order to incorporate as much air as possible into the flour.

Make sure your bowl is large enough to catch the flour.

5 Lightly oil the cake pan. Line the bottom with parchment paper by drawing a pencil around the outside of the pan on the parchment and then cutting it out. Spoon the cake mixture into the prepared pan and smooth the surface with a palette knife.

Why? Smoothing the batter at this stage helps the cake to bake with an even surface, making it easier to frost.

6 Bake the cake in the preheated oven for 45 minutes. Test if the cake is done with a skewer. Also, it should be firm to the touch when gently pressed. Let cool in the pan for 5 minutes. Then move to a wire rack, so air can circulate around the cake, cooling it. Remove the parchment paper.

Remember Let the cake cool in the pan for 5 minutes so it is easier to turn it out of the pan.

A skewer inserted into the center of the cake should come out clean

7 To make the frosting, place the butter, cream cheese, sugar, and vanilla extract in a bowl, and grate in the zest of 1 orange. Using a hand mixer, beat the mixture until you get a smooth and silky mix.

Remember For a smooth frosting, make sure the butter and cream cheese are at room temperature before blending.

Don't grate the bitter white pith, only the orange rind

Spread the frosting over using a swirling motion for added texture

8 To decorate, spread the frosting evenly over the cake with a palette knife. Using a zester, remove long decorative strands of rind from the other orange and sprinkle it around the edge of the cake. You can also use an ordinary grater, but the strands won't be as long.

Tip The frosted cake will keep very well for up to 3 days in an airtight container.

The perfect **Carrot Cake**

Your cake should be firm, well risen, and moist, with evenly dispersed fruit and nuts.

Orange zest is sprinkled in a decorative ring

Frosting is velvety, smooth, and shiny

Crumb is moist, soft, and light

Sides of the cake are firm and dry to the touch

Fruit and nuts are evenly distributed throughout the cake

Did anything go wrong?

The cake is very heavy and dry. You may have overmixed the batter, which causes the gluten in the flour to develop, leading to a dry cake. Next time stop mixing as soon as you're confident the flour is mixed throughout.

There are specks of white flour in the cooked cake. You may not have sifted all lumps out of the flour or been careful enough during the mixing process to ensure no trace of flour remains.

The cake did not rise much. You may have overmixed the batter, knocking the air out of the cake. Mix only until all the ingredients are incorporated and no flecks of flour are visible.

The frosting is running off the top. The cake was not cooled before you spread on the frosting. Next time, be patient and give yourself enough time before frosting.

The frosting is lumpy. The butter and cream cheese may not have been at room temperature before you made the frosting, causing lumps.

Try more Quick Cake recipes ▶ ▶ ▶

Banana Bread

Makes 2 loaves	Bakes in 35–40 minutes	Up to 8 weeks

Ingredients

unsalted butter for greasing

2¾ cups all-purpose flour, plus extra for dusting

2 tsp baking powder

2 tsp cinnamon

1 tsp salt

1 cup (4oz) walnuts, coarsely chopped

3 ripe bananas, mashed

3 large eggs, beaten

finely grated zest and juice of 1 lemon

½ cup vegetable oil

1 cup sugar

½ cup brown sugar

2 tsp pure vanilla extract

Special Equipment

2 x 8½ x 4½ x 2½ (1lb) loaf pans

Preheat the oven to 350°F (180°C). Grease the loaf pans thoroughly and sprinkle 2 tablespoons of flour into each, shaking out any excess.

PREPARE THE BATTER

Sift the flour, baking powder, cinnamon, and salt into a bowl. Mix in the walnuts and make a well in the center. Stir the bananas into the eggs with the lemon zest. Add the oil, sugars, vanilla extract, and lemon juice, and stir. Pour the banana mixture into the well in the flour. Gradually blend the dry ingredients in, stirring until just smooth.

Careful! Do not overmix the batter, otherwise your bread will be heavy.

BAKE THE BREAD

Spoon the batter into the prepared pans, dividing it equally. The pans should be about half full. Smooth over the surface, then bake in the oven for 35–40 minutes. Test each loaf by inserting a skewer into the center. The bread is cooked if it comes out clean. If not clean, return to the oven for another 5 minutes or so, and retest.

Remember When cooked, the loaves will start to shrink away from the sides of the pans.

SERVE THE BREAD

Let the loaves cool slightly in their pans, then transfer to a wire rack to cool completely. To serve, slice the bread and spread with butter or cream cheese. It is also good toasted.

Tip The bread will keep in an airtight container for up to 3 days.

Apple Muffins

Makes 12 | **Bakes in 20–25 minutes** | **Up to 8 weeks**

Ingredients

1 Golden Delicious apple, peeled, cored, and chopped

2 tsp lemon juice

½ cup light brown sugar, plus extra for sprinkling (optional)

1½ cups all-purpose flour

⅔ cup whole-wheat flour

4 tsp baking powder

1 tbsp ground pumpkin pie spice

½ tsp salt

⅓ cup (2oz) pecan nuts, chopped

1 cup milk

¼ cup sunflower oil

1 large egg (room temperature), beaten

Special Equipment

12-hole muffin pan

12 paper muffin liners

Preheat the oven to 400°F (200°C). Line the muffin pan with paper muffin liners.

PREPARE THE BATTER

Place the apple in a bowl with the lemon juice and 4 tablespoons of the sugar, and let soak for 5 minutes. Sift the all-purpose and whole-wheat flours, baking powder, pumpkin pie spice, and salt into a large bowl, adding in any bran left in the sieve. Add the remaining sugar and pecan nuts and make a well in the center. In a liquid measuring cup, mix together the milk, oil, and egg, then stir in the apple mixture. Pour the wet ingredients into the dry ingredients and stir together until just mixed.

Careful! Stir the batter only until just mixed. Overmixing will result in heavy muffins.

Remember The batter will look lumpy at this stage, but this is normal.

BAKE THE MUFFINS

Spoon the batter into the prepared muffin liners, filling each three-quarters full. Bake in the oven for 20–25 minutes or until well risen and golden. Test by inserting a metal skewer into the center of a muffin. If it comes out clean, they are cooked. If not, bake for another few minutes and test again. Let the muffins cool slightly before removing from the pan and transferring to a wire rack to cool completely. Sprinkle with a little extra sugar, if preferred, before serving.

Tip These healthy muffins can be eaten warm or cold. They will keep fresh for up to 2 days if stored in an airtight container.

Ginger Cake

Serves 12

Bakes in 35–45 minutes

Up to 8 weeks

Ingredients

8 tbsp unsalted butter, softened, plus extra for greasing

1 cup corn syrup

½ cup dark brown sugar

¾ cup milk

4 tbsp syrup from preserved ginger jar

finely grated zest of 1 orange

1½ cups self-rising flour

1 tsp baking soda

1 tsp pumpkin pie spice

1 tsp cinnamon

2 tsp ground ginger

4 pieces of preserved ginger, finely chopped and tossed in 1 tbsp all-purpose flour

1 large egg, lightly beaten

Special Equipment

8in (20cm) square cake pan

Preheat the oven to 325°F (160°C). Grease the cake pan and line the bottom with parchment paper.

PREPARE THE BATTER

Put the butter, corn syrup, sugar, milk, and preserved ginger syrup into a saucepan. Heat gently over low heat until the butter has melted and the mixture is smooth and well mixed. Stir in the orange zest, remove from the heat, and let cool slightly for at least 5 minutes.

Sift together the flour, baking soda, pumpkin pie spice, cinnamon, and ground ginger in a large mixing bowl.

Remember By sifting you are not only mixing, but also adding air into the batter, so don't skip this step.

Make a well in the center. Pour the melted mixture into the well and, using a handheld whisk, whisk together until all the ingredients are well mixed. Then stir in the preserved ginger and beaten egg. Pour the batter into the prepared pan.

BAKE AND SERVE

Bake in the preheated oven for 35–45 minutes or until a metal skewer inserted into the center comes out clean. If not, return the cake to the oven, cook for another 5 minutes, and retest. Let the ginger cake cool in its pan for at least 1 hour and then turn onto a wire rack to cool completely.

Why? It's important to leave the cake to cool in its pan so it can firm up, making it less fragile and easier to remove from the pan.

Remove the parchment paper from the cake before cutting into 12 squares and serving.

Tip This cake is very moist and will keep for up to 1 week in an airtight container.

Pecan, Coffee, and Maple Cake

Serves 8

Bakes in 35–40 minutes

Up to 8 weeks

Ingredients

16 tbsp butter, softened, plus extra for greasing

1½ cups self-rising flour

⅔ cup granulated sugar

3 large eggs, at room temperature

4 tbsp espresso, or strong instant coffee

2½oz (75g) pecans, chopped, plus 20 pecan halves to decorate

1 tbsp maple syrup

1⅔ cups confectioners' sugar

Special Equipment

2 x 7in (18cm) round cake pans

Preheat the oven to 350°F (180°C). Lightly grease the cake pans and line their bottoms with a circle of parchment paper.

PREPARE THE BATTER

Sift the flour into a large mixing bowl, then add the sugar, 12 tablespoons of the butter, eggs, and 2 tablespoons of the coffee. Blend the ingredients together using a hand mixer until well mixed.

Remember The mixture should be of "dropping consistency," which means it should easily drop off the beaters when tapped.

Stir in the chopped pecan nuts.

Help! If the mixture seems a little thick, simply stir in a little extra coffee until it reaches the desired consistency.

BAKE THE CAKE

Divide the mixture between the pans, leveling the tops with a spatula or palette knife. Bake for 35–40 minutes or until well risen and firm to the touch. When the cakes are ready, a skewer inserted should come out clean. If not, cook for a few minutes more and retest. Let cool for 5 minutes in their pans, then transfer to a wire rack to cool completely.

DECORATE AND SERVE

To make the icing, melt the remaining butter and maple syrup in a small saucepan. Sift the confectioners' sugar into a bowl, then add the melted butter mixture with the remaining coffee, and mix with the hand mixer until very thick and smooth. Using a spatula or palette knife, spread the coffee icing evenly between the tops of the cooled cakes for a smooth finish, then sandwich together and transfer to a serving plate. Decorate the top with the pecan halves.

Careful! The cakes must be completely cool or the icing will run.

How to make **Cupcakes**

Making small cakes, such as cupcakes, usually requires a very simple technique called "rubbing in." This involves rubbing the fat into the dry ingredients before mixing in the wet ingredients to form a smooth, pourable batter. The rubbing-in process creates light cupcakes that have a soft texture.

Rubbing in the butter

Using your fingertips, rub the butter into the flour until the mixture looks like fine bread crumbs. Rubbing in butter in this manner coats the flour with fat, without melting the butter too much. Coating the flour prevents too much gluten forming when you make the batter (see p.116), which in turn guarantees tender cupcakes.

Keep your palms facing up and use your fingertips to lift and rub the flour and butter together

Pour the same amount of batter into each cupcake liner

Pouring

Once you have added the wet ingredients to the dry mixture, you will have a thick batter. For ease, pour the batter into a liquid measuring cup and pour into paper liners placed in cupcake pans. Fill the cupcake liners half-full so the cupcakes rise evenly and have flat tops. If you overfill them, the edges set faster during baking than the rest of the cupcake, making the cupcakes peak in the middle and crack.

Vanilla Cream Cupcakes

Makes 24

Bakes in 20–25 minutes

4 weeks, unfrosted

Ingredients

1⅓ cups all-purpose flour, sifted

2 tsp baking powder

1 cup sugar

½ tsp salt

7 tbsp unsalted butter, softened

3 large eggs

⅔ cup milk

2 tsp pure vanilla extract

1 cup confectioners' sugar, sifted

cupcake sprinkles, to decorate (optional)

Special Equipment

2 x 12-hole cupcake pans

piping bag and star nozzle (optional)

Preheat the oven to 350°F (180°C).

MAKE THE BATTER

In a bowl, place the flour, baking powder, sugar, salt, and half the butter. Rub in with your fingertips until the mixture resembles bread crumbs. Beat the eggs, milk, and 1 tsp of vanilla extract together until blended. Pour this mixture into the dry ingredients, mixing constantly, until you have a smooth batter. Pour the batter into a liquid measuring cup.

Remember It is very important to make a smooth batter, so always use softened butter and eggs at room temperature for easy mixing.

BAKE THE CUPCAKES

Place the cupcake liners into the cupcake pans, then pour the batter into the liners, filling each only half-full. Bake the cupcakes for 20–25 minutes until

well risen. Insert a metal skewer into the center of each cupcake. If it comes out clean each time, the cupcakes are ready. If not, simply cook for another few minutes and test again. Let the cupcakes cool slightly, then remove them from the pan and transfer to a wire rack to cool completely.

DECORATE AND SERVE

To decorate, beat the confectioners' sugar with the remaining vanilla extract and butter, using a hand mixer, until light and fluffy. Spoon into a piping bag fitted with a star nozzle. Pipe the frosting onto the cupcakes in a spiral pattern, starting at the edge and piping into the center, ending with a peak. Decorate with sprinkles, if preferred.

Tip You can also spoon the frosting on the cupcakes instead of piping. Spread on the frosting using the back of a spoon or a palette knife until smooth.

Chocolate and Lemon Cupcake variations

For chocolate cupcakes, sift 4 tbsp cocoa powder with the flour and stir 1 tbsp Greek yogurt in with the vanilla. For the frosting, substitute 3 tbsp cocoa powder for 3 tbsp confectioners' sugar. For lemon cupcakes, replace the vanilla in the batter with the zest of ½ lemon and juice of 1 lemon. Omit the vanilla in the frosting and add the grated rind of ½ lemon.

How to make **Cookies**

The perfect cookie is golden brown in color, with a soft middle and a slightly crisp outer edge. To achieve a light texture and to make sure that all the cookies in a batch turn out beautifully baked, it's vital to get air into the mix and to roll out the dough into evenly shaped balls.

A properly creamed mixture will be very smooth, light in color, with a slightly increased volume

Beat the butter and sugar together for 2–3 minutes until all the lumps have been smoothed out

Remember You can cream the ingredients by hand as well, using a wooden spoon, but it will take longer.

Creaming

This technique involves beating the butter and sugar together until the mixture is light and fluffy. Creaming causes the sugar crystals to cut into the butter, creating pockets full of air, which will give your cookies a light texture once they are baked.

Make sure the nuts and raisins are thoroughly combined, otherwise your cookies will have uneven amounts of filling ....

.. The dough should be soft but not sticky; add a little milk if too stiff or a little flour if too sticky

Achieving the correct consistency

To ensure a light, soft consistency to your dough, sift in the dry ingredients by holding the sieve high above the bowl and tapping it with your hand until all the flour falls into the bowl. Gently mix the ingredients together to make a dough that is soft but not sticky.

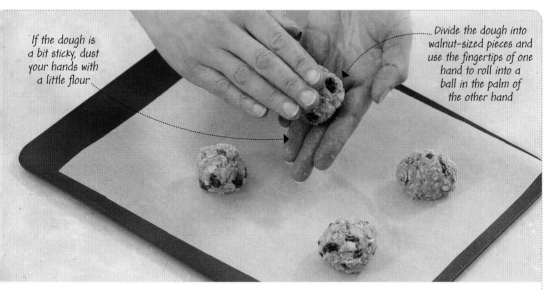

If the dough is a bit sticky, dust your hands with a little flour ..

.... Divide the dough into walnut-sized pieces and use the fingertips of one hand to roll into a ball in the palm of the other hand

Shaping the dough

Dividing and rolling the dough into equal-sized balls is an important part of making cookies. If you divide the dough into balls of varying sizes, you could end up with unevenly baked cookies, with some that are underdone and others that are overcooked.

Hazelnut and Raisin Oat Cookies

For deliciously light and crumbly oat cookies flavored
with raisins and hazelnuts, try this easy cookie recipe.
Perfecting the technique of making and shaping the dough
will give you wonderfully baked cookies every time.

Makes 18 **Bakes in 10–15 minutes** **Up to 8 weeks**

Ingredients

cup (4oz) hazelnuts

tbsp unsalted butter, softened

¼ cups light brown sugar

large egg (room temperature), beaten

tsp pure vanilla extract

tbsp honey

cup self-rising flour, sifted (see p.14)

½ cups oats

tsp salt

cup raisins

little milk, if needed

hazelnuts

unsalted butter

light brown sugar

beaten egg

vanilla extract

honey

self-rising flour

oats

salt

raisins

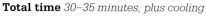

Total time *30–35 minutes, plus cooling*

Prepare
10 minutes

Make
10 minutes

Bake
10–15 minutes

1 Preheat the oven to 375°F (190°C). Toast the hazelnuts on a baking sheet in the oven for 5 minutes, then rub off their skins using a clean dish towel and coarsely chop.

Tip If preferred, and to save time, you can use ready-roasted chopped hazelnuts.

By crisping up the skins in the oven, they should now be easy to rub off

Adding honey will make the cookies extra moist

2 Place the butter and sugar in a large bowl and, using a hand mixer, cream them together until the mixture turns pale and fluffy. Add the egg, vanilla, and honey, and beat again until thoroughly mixed.

Tip Making sure your mixture is pale and fluffy will guarantee smooth-textured cookies.

3 Combine the flour, oats, and salt in a separate bowl, and stir into the mixture. Then stir in the chopped hazelnuts and raisins until everything is combined and distributed evenly.

Remember The cookie dough should be soft enough to shape but not sticky. Add a little extra milk if the mixture is too stiff or flour if too sticky.

Press the cookies down slightly so they cook evenly

Leave enough room for cookies to spread while baking

4 Line a baking sheet with parchment paper. Roll the dough into 18 balls and flatten each slightly on the sheet. Bake in the preheated oven for 10–15 minutes or until golden. Transfer the cookies to a wire rack using a palette knife, and leave to cool.

Remember Try to make the balls as evenly sized as possible, so they cook consistently.

The perfect **Hazelnut and Raisin Oat Cookies**

Your baked cookies should be lightly golden brown, and softer in the middle with a light, chewy texture.

Did anything go wrong?

The cookies are too hard. You have baked them for too long. Remember that they firm up as they cool. Next time check them after 10 minutes and remove from the oven as soon as they look lightly golden.

The cookies are stuck together. The cookies were not spaced out enough prior to baking. Next time, allow more space between cookies for spreading.

Some of the cookies are cooked well, while others are too crispy. The dough was not shaped into evenly sized balls.

The cookies are burned around the edges, but not properly cooked in the center. You did not flatten the cookies enough before baking.

The perfect cookie will have slightly crisp edges and a paler, softer center

Try more Cookie recipes ▶ ▶ ▶

Pistachio and Cranberry Oat Cookies

**Makes
24**

**Bakes in
10–15
minutes**

**Up to
8 weeks**

Ingredients

1 cup (4oz) pistachio nuts

7 tbsp unsalted butter, softened

1¼ cups light brown sugar

1 large egg

1 tsp pure vanilla extract

1 tbsp honey

¾ cup all-purpose flour, sifted

½ tsp baking soda

1½ cups oats

¼ tsp salt

¾ cup (4oz) dried cranberries, coarsely chopped

a little milk, if needed

Preheat the oven to 375°F (190°C). Line 2–3 baking sheets with parchment paper. Dry fry the pistachio nuts in a frying pan over medium heat until lightly colored, taking care not to let them burn. Leave to cool for 1 minute, then coarsely chop.

MAKE THE COOKIE DOUGH

Place the butter and sugar in a bowl and, using a hand mixer, beat until smooth. Add the egg, vanilla extract, and honey, and beat again until smooth. Stir in the flour, baking soda, oats, and salt until well combined. Add the nuts and cranberries and mix.

Help! If the dough is a little too stiff, add a small splash of milk to make it pliable.

SHAPE THE DOUGH

Divide the cookie dough into walnut-sized pieces (the size of whole walnuts, not walnut halves) and roll them into balls. Place on the baking sheets, leaving enough room for the cookies to spread when they cook, and flatten slightly.

Remember If you don't flatten the cookies slightly, they will cook unevenly and brown too much around the edges.

BAKE THE COOKIES

In the preheated oven, bake the cookies in batches, one baking sheet at a time, for 10–15 minutes until golden brown. Leave the cookies on the sheets to cool and firm up slightly. Then, using a palette knife, transfer them to a wire rack to cool completely.

Tip The cookies will keep for up to 5 days if stored in an airtight container.

Apple and Cinnamon Cookies variation
Omit the nuts and cranberries and, after stirring in the flour and oats, add 2 teaspoons cinnamon and 2 peeled, cored, and finely grated apples.

Chocolate Chip Cookies

Makes 30

Bakes in approx. 30 minutes

Up to 8 weeks

Ingredients

14 tbsp unsalted butter, softened

1¼ cups granulated sugar

1 large egg

1 tsp pure vanilla extract

1½ cups self-rising flour

6oz (150g) dark or milk chocolate chips

Preheat the oven to 350°F (180°C). Line 2 baking sheets with parchment paper.

MAKE THE COOKIE DOUGH

Cream the butter and sugar together in a bowl using a hand mixer for 2–3 minutes, until very pale and fluffy.

Remember Creaming brings air into the mix for a lighter cookie, so don't hurry this stage.

Stir in the egg and vanilla extract, then the flour, and beat together until the mixture forms soft dough. Stir in the chocolate chips until well mixed.

Careful! Make sure you mix the chocolate chips evenly throughout the dough so that no cookies are short of chips.

SHAPE THE DOUGH

Divide the cookie dough into walnut-sized pieces (the size of whole walnuts, not walnut halves), shaping in the palms of your hands. Arrange the dough balls on the prepared baking sheets, leaving enough space around each ball, since they spread during baking. Flatten the dough balls very slightly.

Help! If the dough is a little sticky, lightly flour your hands for easier handling.

BAKE THE COOKIES

In the preheated oven, bake the cookies in 2 batches, for 12–15 minutes each or until golden. Let the cookies cool slightly on their baking sheets, then transfer to a wire rack to firm up, using a palette knife, and cool completely.

Remember Don't worry if the cookies are a little soft when you take them out of the oven. They will firm up more on cooling.

Tip These cookies are equally delicious whether served warm or cold. They will keep for up to 5 days if stored in an airtight container.

How to make **Cut-out Cookie Dough**

Cookie dough is simple to make and once mastered, you can cut it into a variety of shapes or add an extra flavoring or two. It's important to achieve a fine consistency when rubbing the butter into the flour and also to roll the dough out into a thin, even layer.

Rub the butter and flour together between your fingertips until the mixture has the consistency of fine bread crumbs

Remember The finer the crumbs, the more tender your cookies will bake.

Use only your fingertips to rub in so that the butter doesn't start melting

Rubbing in

Rubbing the butter into the flour helps to coat the flour particles, which in turn prevents gluten from forming, keeping the cookies deliciously "short," or crisp and crumbly. The dough is then very gently kneaded, just enough to bring it together and smooth out any cracks.

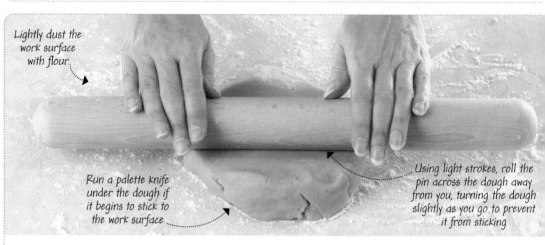

Lightly dust the work surface with flour

Run a palette knife under the dough if it begins to stick to the work surface

Using light strokes, roll the pin across the dough away from you, turning the dough slightly as you go to prevent it from sticking

Rolling out the dough

Scatter flour over the surface and on the rolling pin so the dough doesn't stick. Place the flat of your hands on each end of the rolling pin, then gently roll the dough away from you, using long strokes until the dough is ¼in (5mm) thick all over. This ensures that all cookies bake evenly.

Iow to make **Shortbread**

hortbread is a rich and crumbly type of cookie that can be
1ade into traditional wedges, cookies, or fingers. The high butter
ontent gives shortbread its characteristically crumbly or "short"
exture, and the key to its success is not to overwork the dough.

Making the dough

Since there are no rising
agents in shortbread dough,
you need to cream together
the butter and sugar
(see p.28) in order to
get air into the mixture.
You then gently mix in the
other ingredients to form
a crumbly looking dough.

*Don't overmix,
otherwise the
shortbread will
lose its crumbly
texture and
become tough*

*Don't worry if
your dough is
a bit crumbly
at this stage*

Shaping the dough

When the dough is ready,
shape it into a rough
ball without kneading it.
You want the shortbread
to have a light and crumbly
texture. Kneading would
overwork the gluten in the
flour, making it tough.

Scoring the dough

Once you have pressed
the dough flat in a baking
pan, use a sharp knife to
"score" or lightly mark it
into wedges. This makes
it easier to cut or break the
shortbread into wedges
once it is baked. Then
prick it all over with a fork.

*Pricking
the shortbread
all over allows
steam to escape
as it cooks and
prevents it
from rising
up, leaving a
level surface*

Butter Cookies

To make quick and easy cookies using the
"rubbed in" method, try this simple recipe
for deliciously light and crumbly butter cookies.

Makes 30	**Bakes in 10–15 minutes**	**Unsuitable for freezing**

ngredients

. tbsp unsalted butter, softened
  and cubed

½ cups all-purpose flour, sifted (see p.14),
  plus extra for dusting

cup sugar

large egg yolk

tsp pure vanilla extract

pecial Equipment

¾in (7cm) round cookie cutter

unsalted butter   **all-purpose flour**

sugar   **egg yolk**   **vanilla extract**   **round cookie cutter**

Total time *25–30 minutes, plus cooling*

Prepare
5 minutes

Make
10 minutes

Bake
10–15 minutes

1 Preheat the oven to 350°F (180°C). Using your fingertips, rub together the butter, flour, and sugar, until they resemble fine bread crumbs. Using a wooden spoon, mix in the egg yolk and vanilla extract. You may not need all the egg yolk; use just enough to form a soft, but not sticky, dough.

Tip To save time, pulse the flour and butter in a food processor to form the bread crumbs.

Dough should be soft and still a little crumbly

Do not add too much flour to the surface, since this will make the cookies dry

2 Form the dough into a ball, then turn it onto a lightly floured surface. Knead the dough for a few seconds with the heel of your hand. Push it forward slightly, then fold its far edge into the center. Turn the dough and repeat the process until the dough is smooth.

Help! If your dough is a bit too soft and sticky to roll out, chill it for 15 minutes, and then try again.

3 To roll out the dough, start by slightly flattening it with your hand. Then, using the rolling pin, gently roll it out, without applying too much pressure. Roll the dough only in one direction, away from your body. Continue to roll the dough out to a thickness of ¼in (5mm).

Tip To prevent the dough from sticking to the work surface, run a palette knife under it.

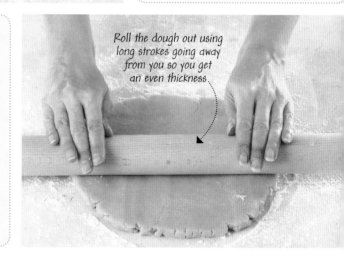

Roll the dough out using long strokes going away from you so you get an even thickness

4 Using a cookie cutter, cut out 30 rounds of the dough, bringing together and rolling any leftover dough again so you get the maximum number of cookies. Place them on baking sheets; you don't need to grease or line the sheets. Bake for 10–15 minutes or until golden brown at the edges. Let cool slightly, then transfer to a wire rack to cool completely.

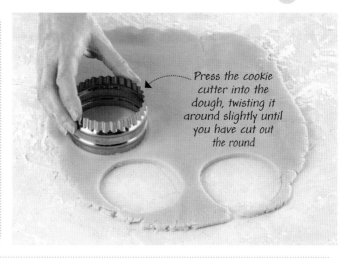

Press the cookie cutter into the dough, twisting it around slightly until you have cut out the round

The perfect **Butter Cookie**

The perfectly baked butter cookie will be lightly golden in color and have a crisp and crumbly texture. They will keep well for up to 5 days if stored in an airtight container.

The cookies should be golden at the edges and slightly paler in the center

Did anything go wrong?

The cookie dough was very sticky. You may have added a little too much egg yolk. Next time, add just enough to bind the ingredients together, and don't be afraid to leave out any surplus.

The cookies have joined at the edges on baking. You may not have left enough space on the baking sheet between the rounds to allow them to spread during baking.

The cookies are very dry. You may have put too much flour on your work surface while rolling out the dough.

The edges of the cookies have browned too much. You may have overcooked them. Next time, take them out of the oven when they start to turn lightly golden at the edges.

You didn't manage to get 30 cookies from the dough. You may not have rolled the dough out thinly enough. Did you remember to roll out any leftover dough?

Try more Cookie recipes ▶▶▶

Gingerbread Men

Makes 16   **Bakes in 10–12 minutes**   **Up to 8 weeks, unbaked**

Ingredients

4 tbsp corn syrup

2⅓ cups all-purpose flour, plus extra for dusting

1 tsp baking soda

1½ tsp ground ginger

1½ tsp pumpkin pie spice

7 tbsp unsalted butter, softened and cubed

¾ cup dark brown sugar

1 large egg

raisins, to decorate

confectioners' sugar, sifted (optional)

Special Equipment

4½in (11cm) gingerbread man cutter

Preheat the oven to 375°F (190°C).

MAKE THE DOUGH

Gently heat the corn syrup in a small saucepan until it is runny, then let it cool slightly.

Careful! Don't neglect to cool the syrup or it will start to cook the egg and melt the butter.

Sift together the flour, baking soda, ginger, and pumpkin pie spice. Add the butter and rub in until it resembles fine bread crumbs (see p.26). Stir in the sugar. Beat the egg into the cooled syrup and pour into the dry ingredients. Mix together with a spoon and then your hands to form dough.

SHAPE THE DOUGH

Briefly knead the dough on a floured surface until smooth. Roll out to ¼in (5mm) thickness.

Careful! Don't put too much flour on your work surface when rolling out the dough, otherwise the cookies will be dry.

Using the cutter, cut out as many gingerbread men as you can. Re-roll the leftover dough and cut out more gingerbread men. Transfer the men to nonstick baking sheets and use raisins to make their eyes, noses, and buttons.

BAKE AND DECORATE

Bake for 10–12 minutes or until golden brown. Cool slightly, then transfer them to a wire rack to cool completely. The gingerbread men will firm up a lot on cooling, so do not overbake them or they will be too crispy.

To decorate, mix a little confectioners' sugar with enough water to form a thin icing. Decorate the men with the icing to make their clothes and bow ties. Let the icing set completely.

Shortbread

Makes 8 triangles

Bakes in 30–40 minutes

Unsuitable for freezing

Ingredients

11 tbsp unsalted butter, softened,
  plus extra for greasing

⅓ cup sugar, plus extra
  for sprinkling

1⅓ cups all-purpose flour

½ cup cornstarch

Special Equipment

8in (20cm) round, loose-bottomed cake pan

Lightly grease and line the pan with parchment paper.

MAKE THE DOUGH

Combine the softened butter and the sugar in a bowl, then cream together using a hand mixer for 2–3 minutes or until very light and fluffy. Sift the flour and cornstarch into the bowl and mix. Using your hands, bring the mixture together to form a dough, then place in the pan.

Remember At this stage, the dough will be slightly crumbly.

Careful! Do not overwork the dough, otherwise your shortbread won't be light and crumbly.

SHAPE THE DOUGH

Press the dough into the pan using your hands, until it fills the pan and is smooth and even on top. Using a sharp knife, lightly score the shortbread into 8 even wedges. Prick the shortbread all over with a fork, then cover it with plastic wrap and chill in the refrigerator for 1 hour. Preheat the oven to 325°F (160°C).

BAKE THE DOUGH

Bake the shortbread in the preheated oven for 30–40 minutes until lightly golden and firm.

Careful! Keep an eye on the shortbread in case it starts to color too much; if it does, lightly cover with foil.

Score the wedges again using a sharp knife while the shortbread is still warm. Sprinkle a dusting of sugar over the top and allow to cool completely. When cool, carefully remove from the pan. Break or cut the shortbread into wedges along the scored lines and serve.

Tip Shortbread will keep well for up to 5 days if stored in an airtight container.

How to make **Meringue**

Meringues are made by beating lots of air into egg whites, then beating in sugar. The mixture is then shaped and baked slowly on low heat so that the moisture in the mixture evaporates, leaving you with crisp meringues that are light as air.

To make sure that your bowl is completely clean, run half a lemon around the bowl before using

Remember to scrape down the sides of the bowl occasionally using a plastic spatula

The egg whites are ready when you lift out the beater and it leaves behind peaks of egg white that hold their shape

Careful! The egg whites must be free from any grease or egg yolk, otherwise they won't beat to a stiff peak. Also take care when separating the eggs so that you don't burst the yolk and contaminate the whites.

Beating the egg whites

For a light and crisp meringue, you must beat your egg whites vigorously using a hand mixer. This stretches the protein in the egg whites, which helps to incorporate air into the mixture and, as a result, increases the volume in the egg whites.

Careful! If you add the sugar before the egg whites are stiff enough, your meringue will end up too soft.

. The beaten egg whites will become smoother and glossier with every addition of sugar

The meringue will form stiff glossy peaks when ready

. Stop beating when your mixture is smooth and glossy

Beating in the sugar

Using a hand mixer, beat in a spoonful of sugar at a time; any quicker and you may deflate the mixture. Make sure to dissolve the sugar into the egg whites by mixing very well after each addition. The mixture will no longer feel grainy when the sugar has fully dissolved. Undissolved sugar attracts moisture, making the meringue soggy.

Strawberry Pavlova

This scrumptious strawberry pavlova combines juicy, sharp strawberries with crisp, sweet meringue. It's an impressive-looking dessert, but easy to make once you've mastered the basic meringue technique. It can also be prepared before a dinner party and assembled just before serving.

1 2 3

erves 8   **Bakes in**   **Unsuitable**
            1 hour 20   **for freezing**
            minutes

ngredients

arge egg whites, at room temperature
....
nch of salt
....
out 1½ cups sugar
(see tip, Step 1)
....
sp cornstarch
....
sp vinegar
....
cups heavy cream
....
awberries, hulled and halved,
:o decorate (or other fruits)
....

egg whites

salt

sugar

cornstarch

vinegar   **heavy cream**   **strawberries**

Total time *1 hour 40 minutes, plus cooling*

Prepare   **Make**   **Bake**   **Decorate**
5 minutes   *10 minutes*   *1 hour 20 minutes*   *5 minutes*

1 Preheat the oven to 350°F (180°C). Line a baking sheet with parchment paper and draw an 8in (20cm) circle with a pencil, using an upturned plate as a guide. Beat the egg whites and salt until they form stiff peaks.

Tip You will need double the weight of sugar to egg whites. Weigh your 6 egg whites and calculate how much sugar you need. The ratio is about 6 egg whites to 1½ cups sugar.

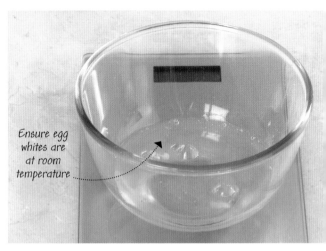

Ensure egg whites are at room temperature

2 Gradually add the sugar, a spoonful at a time, beating well after each addition. Continue beating until the whites are stiff and glossy, then beat in the cornstarch and vinegar.

Why? Cornstarch and vinegar add a softer, chewier texture and stop the egg whites from collapsing.

Careful! Add the sugar gradually, or the meringue will be soft.

Use a glass or metal bowl when making the meringue, since plastic can retain traces of grease

3 Spoon the meringue into a mound inside the circle on the lined baking sheet. First spoon it into the middle, then spread it out to the guideline using a palette knife. Texture the meringue into neat decorative swirls. Bake in the oven for 5 minutes, then reduce to 250°F (130°C) and cook for another 75 minutes until the meringue is crisp and dry. Let cool completely in the oven.

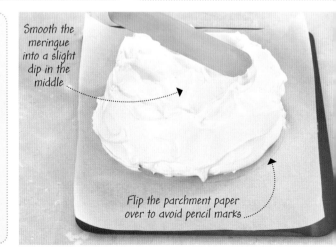

Smooth the meringue into a slight dip in the middle

Flip the parchment paper over to avoid pencil marks

4 Meanwhile, lightly whip the cream using a hand mixer until it just holds its shape. Arrange the cooled meringue on a serving plate, spoon the cream onto the center, leaving a rim around the edge, top with the strawberries, and serve.

Careful! Top the meringue with the cream and strawberries just before you serve, otherwise the meringue will soften.

Whisk the cream until it just forms soft peaks or it will be too firm to spread

The perfect **Strawberry Pavlova**

Your finished pavlova should be crisp and creamy white with a soft and chewy center.

Did anything go wrong?

The egg whites won't beat to a stiff peak. Egg yolk or oil from unwashed cooking equipment has gotten into your egg whites.

The meringue mixture does not have much volume to it. You may have added the sugar before beating the egg whites into stiff peaks.

The meringue has sunk on cooling. It is always best to leave the meringue to cool down completely in the turned-off oven, thus preventing a sudden change in temperature that could cause the meringue to sink or crack.

The meringue has softened. You may have assembled the pavlova too early or spread the cream too widely over the meringue. Next time, assemble just before serving and leave a rim around the edge to prevent the sides from softening and collapsing.

Softly whipped cream

Crisp meringue with few cracks

Try more Meringue recipes ▶ ▶ ▶

Tropical Fruit Pavlova

Serves 8

Bakes in 1 hour 20 minutes

Unsuitable for freezing

Ingredients

6 egg whites, at room temperature (see tip)

pinch of salt

about 1½ cups sugar (see tip)

2 tsp cornstarch

1 tsp vinegar

1¼ cups heavy cream

14oz (400g) mango and papaya, peeled and chopped

2 passion fruits, halved

Preheat the oven to 350°F (180°C). Line a baking sheet with parchment paper and, using a pencil, draw an 8in (20cm) circle on it. Flip the paper over so the pencil does not mark the meringue.

Tip Before you begin to make the pavlova, the best way to ensure good results is to weigh your 6 egg whites and use exactly double the weight of sugar.

MAKE THE MERINGUE

Put the egg whites in a large, clean, grease-free bowl with the salt. Using a hand mixer, beat the egg whites until stiff peaks form. Add the sugar 1 tbsp at a time, beating well after each addition. Continue beating until the mixture becomes very stiff and glossy. Then beat in the cornstarch and vinegar.

Why? Adding cornstarch and vinegar to the mix gives the meringue's center a chewy texture, while its outside remains crisp.

SHAPE AND BAKE THE MERINGUE

Spoon the meringue inside the drawn circle on the parchment paper and spread out with a palette knife. Bake for 5 minutes, then reduce the oven temperature to 250°F (130°C) and cook for 1¼ hours. The meringue is cooked when it is crisp and dry. At this point turn off the oven and, without opening the door, leave the meringue inside until it has cooled completely.

Careful! Don't be tempted to open the oven door before the meringue has cooked, otherwise it will deflate and crack.

DECORATE AND SERVE

Whip the heavy cream in a bowl, using a hand mixer, until it holds its shape. Remove the pavlova from the parchment and arrange on a serving plate. Just before serving, top the pavlova with the whipped cream, then arrange the prepared fruits on top. Spoon the passion fruit juice and seeds over the top to finish, and serve.

Tip The meringue bottom will keep very well if stored in an airtight container for up to 1 week. Always add any toppings to a pavlova just before serving to keep the dessert from becoming soggy.

Rhubarb and Ginger Meringue Cake

Serves 6–8 **Bakes in 1 hour 5 minutes** **Unsuitable for freezing**

Ingredients

4 egg whites, at room temperature

pinch of salt

about 1 cup sugar

1lb 5oz (600g) rhubarb, chopped

4 pieces ginger, chopped

½ tsp ground ginger

1 cup heavy cream

confectioners' sugar, to dust

Preheat the oven to 350°F (180°C). Line 2 baking sheets with parchment paper and draw a 7in (18cm) circle with pencil on each of them. Flip the paper over so the pencil does not mark the meringue.

MAKE THE MERINGUE

Put the egg whites and salt in a large grease-free bowl. Using a hand mixer, beat the egg whites until very stiff peaks form. Add ½ cup of the sugar, 1 tablespoon at a time, beating well after each addition. Continue until all the sugar is incorporated and the mixture is stiff and glossy.

Remember Don't add your sugar before the egg whites are beaten to stiff peaks, otherwise the meringue will be soft.

SHAPE AND BAKE THE MERINGUE

Divide the meringue between the baking sheets and spread out to the circle guidelines. Bake the meringue for 5 minutes, then reduce the oven temperature to 250°F (130°C). Bake for 1 hour, then turn off the oven and leave the meringue to cool completely.

Why? Allowing the meringue to cool slowly in the turned-off oven prevents the meringue from cracking too much.

ASSEMBLE AND SERVE

Put the rhubarb, remaining sugar, ginger, and ground ginger in a saucepan and add just enough water to cover. Cook gently with the lid on for 20 minutes or until soft. Drain off any excess liquid, allow it to cool, and chill until needed. Beat the heavy cream in a bowl, using a hand mixer, until it holds its shape. Then fold in the chilled rhubarb mix. Remove the meringue from the parchment and place one round on a serving plate. Spread the rhubarb and ginger filling on top and place the other meringue over it. Dust the top of the meringue cake liberally with confectioners' sugar. Cut into slices and serve immediately.

Tip The meringue layers will keep very well if stored in an airtight container for up to 5 days. Assemble the cake just before serving to prevent it from becoming soggy.

How to **Pipe Meringue**

You can pipe meringue into rounds, fingers, or even large, flat disks for layered desserts. You can also spoon meringue into your chosen shapes, but piping is faster, gives a more professional finish, and is less messy once you've mastered it. To spoon meringue into shapes, take two dessert spoons, scoop out enough meringue to shape between the spoons, and form the meringue into your desired shape.

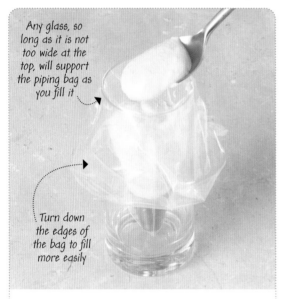

Any glass, so long as it is not too wide at the top, will support the piping bag as you fill it

Turn down the edges of the bag to fill more easily

After piping each round, press down the nozzle very gently into the top of the meringue to prevent it forming a peak

Leave space between each round for spreading

Filling the piping bag

Attach a plain or star nozzle to your piping bag, then place it in a glass for support. Spoon your meringue into the piping bag and, when done, twist the top of the bag to keep the meringue in place.

Piping rounds of meringue

Hold the piping bag with one hand at the top and, using the other hand to guide it, gently squeeze the meringue through the nozzle. Hold the nozzle still until you form a rounded pile of meringue on a lined baking sheet.

Piping meringue into a disk

To create a large, flat disk of meringue, pipe in a spiral, about ½in (1cm) thick. Start from the center and work outward to your required size.

Make a circle guideline on parchment paper and mark a cross at the center of the circle to start from

Raspberry Cream Meringues

**Makes
6–8**

**Bakes in
1 hour**

**Unsuitable
for freezing**

Ingredients

4 egg whites (room temp); each weighs about 1oz

about 1 cup sugar (see tip)

4oz (100g) raspberries

1 cup heavy cream

1 tbsp confectioners' sugar, sifted

Special Equipment

piping bag and plain nozzle

Preheat the oven to 250°F (130°C). Line
2 baking sheets with parchment paper.

Tip For best results, weigh the egg whites and
calculate how much sugar you need. You will
need double the weight of sugar to egg whites.

WHISK THE MERINGUE

Put the egg whites in a large, clean, grease-free
bowl and, using a hand mixer, beat the egg whites
until very stiff peaks form. Gradually add half the
sugar, a couple of tablespoons at a time, beating
well after each addition. Gently fold in the
remaining sugar until all is incorporated.

Careful! Make sure the sugar is beaten in
gradually, otherwise the meringue will be soft.

SHAPE AND BAKE

Pipe rounds onto the lined baking sheets
using the piping bag fitted with a plain
nozzle. Leave a 2in (5cm) gap between each
round. Alternatively, spoon teaspoons of the
mixture onto the sheets. Bake in the preheated
oven for 1 hour. Turn off the heat and leave the
meringues inside the oven to cool completely,
keeping the door shut.

Remember The meringues will be crisp and dry
when baked and should sound hollow when tapped
on the bottom.

FILL AND SERVE

Crush the raspberries with a fork in a bowl.
Beat the heavy cream in another bowl using a
hand mixer until it holds its shape and then stop,
since you don't want to overbeat it. Gently fold the
crushed raspberries and confectioners' sugar into
the cream until well mixed. When ready to serve,
spread a little of the raspberry mixture onto half of
the meringues. Top with remaining meringues and
press together. Serve immediately.

Tip Unfilled meringues will keep very well for up
to 5 days if stored in an airtight container. Always
assemble the meringues just before serving to
keep them from becoming soggy.

Brown Sugar Meringues

Makes 18 | **Bakes in 1 hour** | **Unsuitable for freezing**

Ingredients

4 egg whites at room temperature

1 cup brown sugar

1¼ cups heavy cream

3oz (85g) dark chocolate, broken into pieces

Special Equipment

piping bag and plain nozzle

Preheat the oven to 250°F (130°C). Line 2 baking sheets with parchment paper.

MAKE THE MERINGUE

Put the egg whites in a large, clean, grease-free bowl. Beat the egg whites, using a hand mixer, until very stiff peaks form.

Careful! Always make sure your bowl and beaters are totally free from any grease or egg yolk. Even a tiny trace could prevent the air from being incorporated properly and stop the egg whites from beating up enough.

Gradually add the sugar, 2 tablespoons at a time, and beat well after each addition, until all is incorporated. Continue to beat until the mixture is very thick and glossy.

SHAPE AND BAKE

Pipe rounds onto the lined baking sheets using the piping bag fitted with a plain nozzle. Leave a 2in (5cm) gap between each round. Alternatively, spoon teaspoons of the mixture onto the sheets. You should end up with 36 meringues. Bake in the preheated oven for 1 hour. To make sure the meringues stay crisp, turn off the oven and leave the meringues to cool inside. Then transfer them to a wire rack to cool completely.

Remember The meringues will be crisp and dry when cooked and should sound hollow when tapped on the bottom.

DECORATE AND SERVE

Beat the heavy cream in a bowl, using a hand mixer, until it holds its shape. Melt the chocolate until smooth in a heatproof bowl set over a pan of simmering water.

Careful! Do not let the bottom of the bowl containing the chocolate touch the water, otherwise the chocolate will overheat and become grainy.

When ready to serve, spread a little of the whipped cream onto half of the meringues. Top with the remaining half of the meringues and press together. Arrange the brown sugar meringues on a serving plate. Using a teaspoon, carefully drizzle a little of the melted chocolate over each meringue and serve immediately.

Pistachio Meringues

Makes 8 | **Bakes in 1½ hours** | **Unsuitable for freezing**

Ingredients

4oz (100g) unsalted, shelled pistachio nuts

4 egg whites, at room temperature

about 1 cup sugar (see tip)

Preheat the oven to 250°F (130°C). Line a baking sheet with parchment paper.

Tip For best results, weigh the egg whites and calculate how much sugar is needed. You will need double the weight of sugar to egg whites.

PREPARE THE NUTS

Put the pistachio nuts on an unlined baking sheet and bake for 5 minutes, then place on a clean dish towel and rub to remove their skins. Finely grind half the nuts in a food processor and roughly chop the rest.

BEAT THE MERINGUE

Put the egg whites in a large, clean, grease-free bowl and, using a hand mixer, beat until very stiff peaks form. Gradually add the sugar, 1 tablespoon at a time, beating well after each addition, until half of the sugar is incorporated. Fold in the remaining sugar and ground pistachio nuts very carefully.

Remember Fold in the sugar and ground pistachio nuts very carefully making sure you do not knock any air out of the mixture, which could deflate the meringue.

SHAPE AND BAKE

Place heaping tablespoons of the meringue onto the lined baking sheet, leaving plenty of space between them, since they will spread as they bake.

Scatter the tops with the chopped pistachio nuts. Bake the meringues for 1½ hours, or until crisp and dry, then turn off the oven and leave the meringues inside to cool completely. This will help to minimize the amount of cracking.

Tip These meringues will keep very well if stored in an airtight container for up to 3 days.

How to make **No-Bake Cheesecake**

No baking is required for these quick cheesecakes, since the cream cheese filling is set with gelatin. Gelatin is an easy-to-use gelling agent made from animal protein, which is supplied in powdered form or in transparent leaves. The velvety texture of the topping, beaten until very smooth, contrasts beautifully with the crispy crumb base.

Vanilla wafers or graham crackers must be finely crushed or the base will break up easily and won't support the cheesecake

Press down the crumb mixture firmly with the back of a spoon to form an even base

Tip You can use graham crackers, vanilla wafers, or most cookies for the base. To save time, crush them in a food processor.

Making the base

The classic base is made by mixing crushed graham crackers or vanilla wafers with melted butter, then pressing the mixture into the pan. On chilling, the butter solidifies and binds the crumbs into a base that supports the filling. To make the base, place the crackers or wafers in a freezer bag. Crush them with a rolling pin until they resemble bread crumbs (see p.106).

Tip The gelatin must be completely dissolved before use, otherwise it won't set the filling. Gelatin comes in powdered form or as leaf gelatin. Both are prepared by dissolving in water.

Dissolving the gelatin

Leaf gelatin must be cut into pieces and soaked in a liquid before use. This softens the gelatin, allowing it to absorb water and dissolve fully when melted over a pan of simmering water. As it melts, stir until no traces of the gelatin are visible. Cool for 3–5 minutes before adding to the filling. The gelatin will then re-form into a gel that sets the topping.

Dissolved gelatin will form a clear, smooth liquid

Making the filling

A typical filling is a mixture of whipped cream and cream cheese or similar alternatives such as mascarpone or ricotta cheese. The key to a great filling is to beat the cream cheese until very smooth and then gently fold in the whipped cream using a figure-eight movement, to make sure you don't lose any volume.

Ensure the cream cheese is at room temperature before beating for a lump-free filling

Lemon Cheesecake

Try this simple but luscious lemon cheesecake recipe.
It combines a perfectly smooth filling on a crispy base.
An all-time favorite, it can be made in advance and is ideal
for any dinner party or family get-together.

Serves 8 **Sets in 4 hours** **Unsuitable for freezing**

vanilla wafers

unsalted butter

ngredients

oz (250g) vanilla wafers

tbsp unsalted butter

sheets gelatin or 1 tbsp powdered gelatin

nely grated zest and juice of 2 lemons

2oz (350g) cream cheese, at room
   temperature

 cup sugar

¼ cups heavy cream

gelatin sheets

lemon zest and juice

cream cheese

pecial Equipment

in (23cm) round springform cake pan

sugar

heavy cream

springform cake pan

Total time *35 minutes, plus minimum 4 hours chilling*

Prepare
5 minutes

Make
30 minutes

Set
4 hours or overnight

1 Line the pan with parchment paper. Place the cookies or crackers in a freezer bag and crush to fine crumbs with a rolling pin. Melt the butter in a small saucepan. Stir the crumbs into the butter until well mixed, then firmly press the mixture into the base of the pan.

Tip If the crumb mixture looks a little dry and is not binding together enough, simply add a little more melted butter.

Crush the cookies or crackers into fine, even-sized crumbs to ensure a firm base to the cheesecake

Slightly chill the gelatin once it has melted

2 Soak the gelatin in the lemon juice for 5 minutes. Melt it in a bowl set over a pan of simmering water. Remove from the heat and cool for 3–5 minutes. With a hand mixer, beat together the cream cheese, sugar, and lemon zest until very smooth, making sure there are no lumps.

Tip It is best to mix in softened cheese—simply remove from the fridge about an hour before using.

3 Clean the beater attachments, then beat the heavy cream in a bowl until it forms soft peaks. Beat the gelatin into the cream cheese mixture until well mixed, then carefully fold the heavy cream into this mix using a figure-eight motion.

Careful! Fold the whipped cream in very gently, making sure you don't lose any volume.

It is easiest to fold the cream in gently using a spatula

4 Spoon the filling into the prepared cake pan, smoothing the surface so it is flat and even. Chill for 4 hours or overnight until firm. To release the cheesecake, unclip the sides of the pan and push the bottom up. Transfer it to a serving plate. Remove the metal bottom and parchment paper.

Tip Run a knife around the edge of the cheesecake before releasing it from the pan so it doesn't stick.

The perfect **Lemon Cheesecake**

Your lemon cheesecake should be set firm, with a light creamy texture and a crisp base. If you like, decorate with strands of lemon zest using a zester.

The base is compact, even, and not too crumbly

Cream cheese topping is light and lump-free

Did anything go wrong?

The cheesecake is too soft. You may not have chilled it long enough to allow the gelatin to set. For best results, chill the cheesecake overnight.

The cheesecake has a lumpy texture. The cream cheese was not softened enough before you beat it in with the other ingredients. Next time, make sure you take it out of the fridge at least an hour before using it.

The base is too crumbly. You may not have mixed in enough butter, which binds the crumbs together, or crushed the crumbs finely enough. Next time, crush the cookies or crackers to a fine, uniform size and make sure to coat the crumbs completely with butter, adding more if needed.

Try more No-bake Cheesecake recipes ▶ ▶ ▶

Cherry Cheesecake

Serves 6 · **Sets in 2 hours** · **Unsuitable for freezing**

Ingredients

5 tbsp unsalted butter, plus extra for greasing

7oz (200g) vanilla wafers, finely crushed

2 x 8oz (250g) tubs ricotta cheese

¼ cup sugar

finely grated zest and juice of 2 lemons

½ cup heavy cream

1 tbsp powdered gelatin

14oz (400g) can black cherries or morello cherries in juice

Special Equipment

8in (20cm) round springform cake pan

Grease and line the bottom of the springform cake pan with parchment paper.

MAKE THE CHEESECAKE

Melt the butter in a saucepan and stir in the crushed cookie crumbs until well mixed. Spoon into the prepared pan, pressing down firmly, and transfer to the fridge.

Beat together the ricotta, sugar, and lemon zest until smooth.

Beat the heavy cream in a separate bowl until it forms soft peaks. Stir the cream into the cheese mixture.

Meanwhile, mix the lemon juice and gelatin in a small bowl, then heat gently over a saucepan of simmering water until the gelatin has dissolved, making sure not to boil the mixture, since this can destroy the gelatin. Remove from the heat and cool slightly. Then slowly pour the dissolved gelatin into the cheese mixture, stirring until well mixed. Spoon the cheesecake filling into the base, smoothing over the surface. Chill in the fridge for 2 hours or until set and firm.

DECORATE AND SERVE

Bring the cherry juice to a boil in a saucepan and simmer until reduced by three-quarters and syrupy. Leave to cool. To serve the cheesecake, carefully remove it from the pan and arrange on a serving plate.

Careful! It's best to run a palette knife around the edge of the cheesecake before removing it from the pan to prevent cracking.

Arrange the cherries on top, spoon over the sauce, and serve in slices.

Strawberry Cheesecake

Serves | **Chill for** | **Unsuitable**
8–10 | 1 hour | for freezing

Ingredients

4 tbsp unsalted butter

4oz (100g) good-quality dark chocolate,
    broken into pieces

6oz (150g) vanilla wafers, crushed (about 41 cookies)

14oz (400g) mascarpone cheese,
    at room temperature

finely grated zest and juice of 2 limes

2–3 tbsp confectioners' sugar, plus extra for dusting

8oz (225g) strawberries, hulled and halved

Special Equipment

8in (20cm) round springform cake pan

Line the bottom of the cake pan with parchment paper and set aside.

FORM THE BASE

Melt the butter and chocolate until smooth in a heatproof bowl set over a pan of simmering water (see p.96). Stir the melted mixture into the cookie crumbs, then spoon into the pan, pressing the mixture down with a spoon until even. Chill in the fridge.

MAKE THE CHEESE FILLING

Beat the mascarpone in a bowl with the lime zest (saving a little for decoration), lime juice, and confectioners' sugar to taste. Spoon over the cake base into the pan, smooth over the surface, and chill for 1 hour or until firm.

Remember Since gelatin is not used to set this cheesecake, make sure it is chilled well until firm enough to cut into slices.

DECORATE AND SERVE

To serve, **carefully remove** the cheesecake from the pan and arrange on a serving plate. Place the halved strawberries around the edge, the reserved lime zest in the middle, and dust with confectioners' sugar. Serve in slices.

Tip You can also use graham crackers or other cookies in place of vanilla wafers. For an extra chocolatey base, try chocolate chip cookies. Ginger snaps are another good alternative.

How to use **Store-bought Pastry**

As an alternative to making your own pastry, you can also use store-bought pastry. Both pie dough and puff pastry can be found refrigerated in sheets or blocks to be rolled out or frozen in pie pans ready to be filled and baked. Think of it as a real time-saver and not cheating—even experienced chefs use store-bought puff pastry instead of making it from scratch.

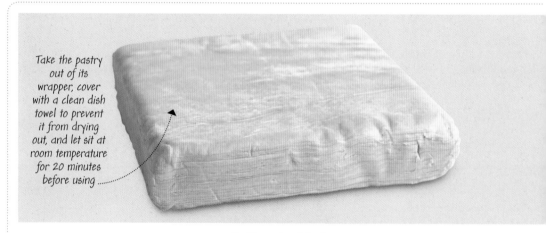

Take the pastry out of its wrapper, cover with a clean dish towel to prevent it from drying out, and let sit at room temperature for 20 minutes before using

Puff pastry block

Keep the puff pastry rolled up until you want to use it—that way it doesn't dry out

Leave at room temperature for 20 minutes before using, since this keeps the pastry from cracking when you roll it out

Ready-rolled puff pastry

Buying pastry

You can buy standard ready-made pie dough and puff pastries as well as "all-butter" variations, which have a higher percentage of butter to give a superior, melt-in-your-mouth taste. Both variations deliver consistent results on baking, but for extra flavor the all-butter pastry is recommended. All types of pastry, block or ready-rolled, are suitable for freezing.

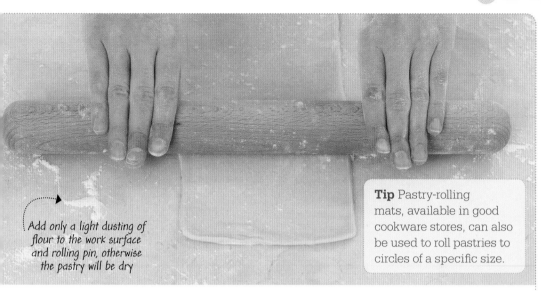

Add only a light dusting of flour to the work surface and rolling pin, otherwise the pastry will be dry

Tip Pastry-rolling mats, available in good cookware stores, can also be used to roll pastries to circles of a specific size.

Rolling out the pastry

Place the unwrapped pastry on a lightly floured surface. With a lightly floured rolling pin, roll it out in long, even strokes away from you. Rotate it by 45° between strokes. For tarts and pies, the pastry is usually rolled out to ¼in (5mm) thick, but always refer to your recipe.

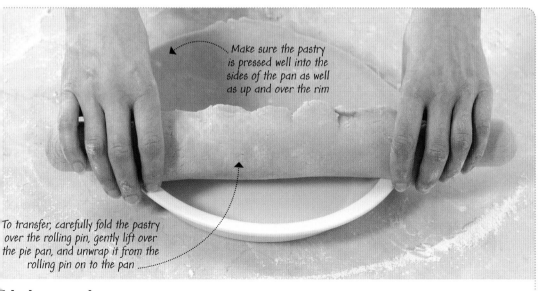

Make sure the pastry is pressed well into the sides of the pan as well as up and over the rim

To transfer, carefully fold the pastry over the rolling pin, gently lift over the pie pan, and unwrap it from the rolling pin on to the pan

Lining a pie pan

Roll out your pastry 2in (5cm) larger than your pie or tart pan. With a rolling pin, lift the pastry, drape it over the pie pan, and press into the bottom and sides. Trim off any excess pastry using a knife. Chill for 30 minutes to relax the pastry and so prevent shrinkage on baking.

Steak and Wild Mushroom Pie

Now you are armed with all the top tips for using store-bought pastry, try this classic pie that's guaranteed to impress your guests. We'll show you how to make the perfect puff pastry lid—one that doesn't turn soggy during baking—along with how to create a decorative edge.

Serves 4–6	**Bakes in 25–35 minutes**	**Unsuitable for freezing**

Ingredients

4lb (1kg) sirloin steak, cut into 1in (2.5cm) cubes

cup all-purpose flour

2oz (500g) mixed fresh wild mushrooms, wiped with a soft clean cloth and sliced

shallots, finely chopped

cups beef stock, plus extra if needed

lt and freshly ground black pepper

parsley sprigs, leaves finely chopped

2oz (500g) store-bought puff pastry

arge egg, beaten, for egg wash

Special Equipment

quart pie dish

sirloin steak

all-purpose flour

fresh wild mushrooms

shallots

beef stock

parsley sprigs

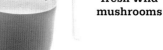

pie dish

beaten egg

salt and pepper

puff pastry

pie dish

Total time *3 hours–3 hours 40 minutes*

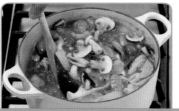

Prepare
5 minutes

Make *2½–3 hours, includes cooking the stew*

Bake
25–35 minutes

1 Preheat the oven to 350°F (180°C). Toss the steak in the flour. Place the steak, mushrooms, shallots, and stock in a casserole dish. Bring to a boil. Cover and bake in the oven for 2–2¼ hours, until the meat is tender and the sauce thick. Adjust the seasoning, stir in the parsley, and transfer to the pie dish.

Why? Toss the steak in seasoned flour so the sauce thickens up.

The sauce should be rich and thick or it will make the pastry soggy

To help bring the filling mixture to a boil quickly, add hot stock

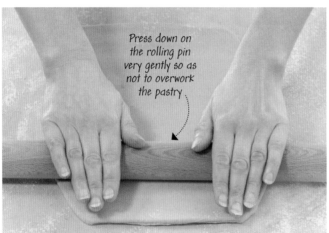

Press down on the rolling pin very gently so as not to overwork the pastry

2 Increase the oven temperature to 425°F (220°C). Roll out the pastry on a lightly floured surface until ¼in (5mm) thick and about 2in (5cm) bigger than the pie dish all around.

Remember To ensure an even thickness, roll the pastry away from you using long strokes and rotating the pastry 45° after each roll.

3 Cut a thin strip from the rolled out pastry. Moisten the rim of the pie dish with cold water and place the pastry on to it. Brush the pastry rim with a little egg and top with the remaining dough, trimming off excess pastry.

Help! If your sauce is too runny, drain it off from the meat into a pan and boil rapidly until thickened and reduced slightly.

The strip of pastry around the rim sticks to the pastry lid and stops it from sliding into the pie

4 Firmly press the pastry lid onto the rim to seal. Flute the edge of the pastry by pressing a finger into the pastry and drawing the back of a knife inward to make a short groove. Brush the lid with egg wash to give it a nice glaze when baked. Make a ½in (1cm) hole in the lid to allow the steam to escape while baking. Chill the pie for 15 minutes to relax the pastry and prevent it from shrinking, then bake for 25–35 minutes.

Pushing down the edges with your finger will also join the two layers of pastry together

The perfect **Steak and Wild Mushroom Pie**

Your finished pie should have a crisp, flakey, golden-brown top and a filling that is deliciously moist.

Did anything go wrong?

The pastry has sunk. There may not have been enough filling to support the pastry lid, or there was too much liquid in the filling, or the pie dish was too large.

The pastry has not risen and is soggy. The oven must be preheated to 425°F (220°C) so the pastry cooks quickly before it becomes soggy.

The pie filling has escaped from the pie dish and leaked everywhere. In this case, your pie dish may not have been large enough, causing the filling to boil over when baked.

The pastry has browned too much before cooking through and rising properly. Your rolled-out pastry may have been too thick. Next time, make sure it's no thicker than ¼in (5mm).

Pastry is golden brown, crisp, and cooked through

Filling is rich and thick, not runny

Try more Store-bought Pastry bakes ▶ ▶ ▶

Fish and Leek Pie

**Serves
4**

**Bakes in
20–30
minutes**

**3 months,
unbaked**

Ingredients

1 tbsp olive oil

1 onion, finely chopped

salt and freshly ground black pepper

4 leeks, finely sliced

1 tsp all-purpose flour

⅔ cup hard cider

2 tbsp flat-leaf parsley, chopped

⅔ cup heavy cream

1½lb (675g) raw white fish, such as haddock,
  cod, or pollack, cut into chunks

10oz (300g) store-bought puff pastry

1 large egg, beaten, for egg wash

Special Equipment

1 quart pie dish

Preheat the oven to 400°F (200°C).

MAKE THE FILLING

Heat the oil in a large frying pan, add the
onion and salt, and fry gently for 4–5 minutes, until
soft and translucent. Add the leeks to the pan and
cook gently for 8–10 minutes, until softened. Stir in
the flour, adding a little of the cider first to make a
smooth paste, then gradually stir in the remaining
cider to make a smooth sauce, and cook for
5–8 minutes, or until thickened.

Careful! Make sure the sauce in the filling has
thickened sufficiently before adding the fish,
otherwise it can make the pastry soggy.

Stir the chopped parsley, cream, and fish into
the leek mixture until well mixed. Season with salt
and pepper. Spoon the filling into the pie dish.

TOP AND BAKE THE PIE

Roll out the pastry on a lightly floured surface
until it is 2in (5cm) bigger than the pie dish. Cut
a strip of pastry about ½in (1cm) wide all around to
form the pastry rim and use this to edge the dish,
fixing it with a little water.

Why? It's best to add a rim of pastry to the pie
dish before topping with the lid to prevent the
lid from sliding into the filling.

Brush the pastry rim with egg wash, then
top with the pastry lid, trimming off any excess.
Pinch the edges together to seal and cut 2 steam
vents in the top of the pie with a knife. Brush the
top of the pie liberally with the egg wash, then
bake in the preheated oven for 20–30 minutes, or
until the pastry is well risen and golden brown.
Serve hot.

Sausage Rolls

**Makes
24**

**Bakes in
10–12
minutes**

**Up to 12
weeks,
unbaked**

Ingredients

10oz (300g) store-bought puff pastry

all-purpose flour, for dusting

1½lb (675g) sausage meat

1 small onion, finely chopped

1 tbsp thyme leaves

1 tbsp finely grated lemon zest

1 tsp Dijon mustard

1 large egg yolk

salt and freshly ground black pepper

1 egg, beaten, for glazing

PREPARE THE PASTRY

Cut the pastry in half lengthwise, then on a
lightly floured surface roll out each half to form
a rectangle 12 x 6in (30 x 15cm). Cover with plastic
wrap and chill for 30 minutes. Preheat the oven
to 400°F (200°C). Line a baking sheet with
parchment paper and chill.

Why? Chilling the pastry prevents it from
shrinking too much while baking.

MAKE THE FILLING

In a bowl, combine the sausage meat,
chopped onion, thyme, lemon zest, mustard, and
egg yolk, and season to taste. Use your hands to
mix the ingredients thoroughly, then divide into
2 equal amounts.

SHAPE AND BAKE THE ROLLS

Shape the sausage meat into 2 equal lengths,
each long enough to be placed down the center
of the rolled-out puff pastry. Place the filling on
the pastry, brush the edges of the pastry with

egg, and fold over to enclose the sausage filling.
Press the edges together to seal, then cut each
roll into 12 pieces. Arrange on the chilled baking
sheet, cut a slash in the top of each roll, and brush
with beaten egg.

Why? Cutting a slash in the top of each roll will
allow the steam to escape as it bakes, preventing
the pastry from becoming soggy.

Bake the sausage rolls in the oven for
10–12 minutes, or until the pastry is well risen
and golden brown. Serve warm or transfer to
a wire rack to cool completely.

How to make **Quick Breads**

Quick breads, as the name suggests, take no time at all to make. The dough for these breads requires very little kneading, and, since yeast is not used, the breads don't need to be left to rise or "prove." To make the breads rise, you replace the yeast with other rising agents, such as baking powder, baking soda, or self-rising flour.

Buttermilk is found in the dairy section of supermarkets

Make a well in the center of your ingredients, add the buttermilk, and gradually draw the dry ingredients into the buttermilk

Adding the buttermilk

Many quick breads use baking soda as their rising agent, and for it to work well, you need to mix it with buttermilk. Buttermilk is a thick and creamy liquid, these days made by fermenting milk with lactic acid cultures. The buttermilk's acid reacts with the baking soda to produce bubbles of carbon dioxide, making for light, well-risen breads.

It is normal for quick breads to have a slightly sticky dough

Make sure your surface is well dusted with flour

Bringing the dough together

Using lightly floured hands to prevent sticking, bring all the ingredients together until they form a rough dough, and shape into a ball.

At this stage, the dough is likely to be sticky. Don't worry about overflouring the work surface, since this won't dry out your breads.

Push the dough forward with your knuckles, then fold it back on itself

Hold an end of the dough with one hand

Gently pat the dough into a round, smoothing over the surface

Kneading and shaping

Knead only to smooth out the dough, since the chemical rising agents will do most of the work in getting the bread to rise. As soon

as you have kneaded your dough, you need to shape it and bake it, since the rising agents will start to work right away.

Soda Bread

Now that you know how effortless it is to make quick
breads, try out this recipe for a quick and easy
soda bread that requires no kneading at all.

Makes 1
loaf

Bakes in
35–40
minutes

✳

Unsuitable
for
freezing

ngredients

:ups whole-wheat bread flour, preferably
stone-ground, plus extra for dusting

tsp baking soda

tsp salt

:ups buttermilk, plus
extra if needed

salted butter, for greasing

whole-wheat bread flour

baking soda

buttermilk

salt

**unsalted
butter**

Total time *50–55 minutes, plus cooling*

Prepare
5 minutes

Make
10 minutes

Bake
35–40 minutes

Work quickly to make a soft, slightly sticky, dough

1 Preheat the oven to 400°F (200°C). Sift together the flour, baking soda, and salt into a bowl, adding any leftover bran from the sieve. Make a well in the flour mix and pour buttermilk into the center, drawing in the flour to make a soft dough.

Tip It's best to use your hands to mix the bread dough, since this will prevent it from overworking.

2 You should have a soft dough, but add a little extra buttermilk if it's too dry. Different flours will have slightly different absorbency levels, even between batches of the same flour. Turn the dough onto a floured surface and shape it into a round loaf.

Careful! If you overwork the dough, you will end up with a heavy loaf.

Shape just enough to get a smoothish dough, which may have some cracks

Cut a cross ½in (1cm) deep in the top of the loaf

3 Grease a baking sheet with the butter. Place the dough on it, shaping it and patting it down into a round approximately 2in (5cm) high. Using a sharp knife, cut a cross in the top of the loaf.

Why? Cutting a cross in the top of the dough makes it easier for the dough to expand, which helps the loaf rise up evenly on baking.

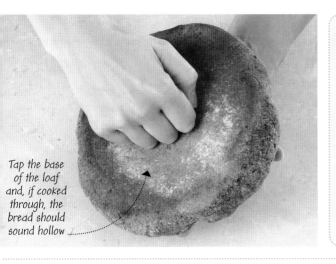

Tap the base of the loaf and, if cooked through, the bread should sound hollow

4 Bake the loaf for 35–40 minutes until it is well browned. Cool slightly on a wire rack—this allows the air to circulate freely around the loaf, preventing moisture from being trapped underneath, which would make the bread soggy.

Tip This bread is best served warm, but will keep for 1–2 days in an airtight container.

The perfect **Soda Bread**

Your perfect soda bread will look golden brown, be well risen, and have a very light, almost cakelike texture.

The loaf has risen evenly

The crust has a slight crunch to it without being too dry

The "crumb" of the bread has a soft, light texture

Did anything go wrong?

The center of the loaf feels damp. You haven't cooked the loaf for long enough. It should be completely dry in the center.

The loaf has risen unevenly. You didn't sift the dry ingredients together properly, resulting in uneven dispersal of the rising agent.

The soda bread is very dry. You have overbaked the loaf or kept it for too long—it really only keeps for a few days.

The outside crust of the soda bread is dry and hard. You may have baked the bread for too long, resulting in a hard crust. Next time, check the loaf after 35 minutes and if it sounds hollow when tapped on the bottom it is cooked through.

Try more Quick Bread recipes ▶ ▶ ▶

Pumpkin Bread

| **Makes 1 loaf** | **Bakes in 50 minutes** | **Up to 8 weeks** |

Ingredients

1¾ cups all-purpose flour, plus extra for dusting

¾ cup whole-wheat flour

1 tsp baking soda

½ tsp fine salt

5oz (120g) pumpkin or butternut squash, peeled, seeded, and coarsely grated

½ cup pumpkin seeds

1¼ cups buttermilk

Preheat the oven to 425°F (220°C). Line a baking sheet with parchment paper.

MAKE THE DOUGH

Sift together the flours, baking soda, and salt in a bowl. Add the grated pumpkin and seeds and mix well. Make a well in the center and pour in the buttermilk.

Why? Combining baking soda and buttermilk creates a reaction, producing carbon dioxide, which acts as the bread's rising agent.

Stir together until it combines to form a sticky dough. Turn the dough out onto a lightly floured surface and knead lightly for 2 minutes until it is smooth.

Help! If you find the dough is too sticky to knead, add a little extra flour.

SHAPE AND BAKE THE BREAD

Shape the dough into a 6in (15cm) round and place on the baking sheet. Using a sharp knife, slash a cross in the top of the bread to help it rise when baking.

Bake in the preheated oven for 30 minutes until risen, then reduce the oven temperature to 400°F (200°C). Bake for another 20 minutes or until cooked through. The bottom of the bread should sound hollow when tapped. Remove from the oven and cool slightly. Then transfer to a wire rack to cool for at least 20 minutes before serving. Cut the bread into slices or wedges and serve.

Tip This bread will keep for up to 3 days if wrapped well in paper.

Cornbread

Serves 8

Bakes in 20–25 minutes

Unsuitable for freezing

Ingredients

4 tbsp unsalted butter, or bacon dripping for extra flavor, melted and cooled, plus extra for greasing

2 fresh corn cobs, to yield about 7oz (200g) kernels

1½ cups fine yellow cornmeal or polenta

¾ cup bread flour

¼ cup sugar

1 tbsp baking powder

1 tsp salt

2 eggs

1¼ cups milk

Special Equipment

9in (23cm) flameproof cast-iron frying pan, or similar-sized loose-bottomed round cake pan

Preheat the oven to 425°F (220°C). Grease the pan with butter or dripping and preheat the pan in the oven.

MAKE THE BATTER

Holding the corn cobs upright, carefully cut the kernels from the cobs using a sharp knife. Then scrape out any remaining pulp from the cobs with the back of a knife and add to the kernels.

Tip If fresh corn on the cob is not available, simply use 7oz (200g) drained canned corn kernels instead.

Sift together the cornmeal or polenta, flour, sugar, baking powder, and salt into a large bowl. Stir in the corn. In a separate bowl, beat together the eggs, melted butter or bacon dripping, and

milk. Pour three-quarters of the milk mixture into the flour mixture and stir, drawing in the dry ingredients. Add the remaining milk mixture and stir until just well mixed.

Careful! Do not overmix or the cornbread may be tough.

BAKE THE BREAD

Using oven gloves, carefully take the preheated pan out of the oven and pour in the batter. Don't worry if it sizzles—this is normal. Quickly brush the top with the butter or bacon dripping. Bake in the oven for 20–25 minutes. When ready, the cornbread should shrink away slightly from the sides of the pan, and a skewer inserted into it should come out clean. Remove from the oven and let the bread cool slightly in the pan on a wire rack.

Cut the bread into wedges and serve while still warm, since it does not keep very well.

2

Build On It

Now you can build on the techniques you've learned with recipes that require slightly more skill. Learn how to make classic creamed cakes, melt-in-your-mouth brownies, pie dough for savory or sweet pies and tarts, as well as how to prepare the yeast and knead the dough for perfectly risen bread.

In this section, learn to bake:

Creamed Cakes
pp.82–95

Brownies
pp.96–105

Baked Cheesecake
pp.106–13

Tarts & Pies
pp.114–31

Yeast-risen Breads
pp.132–45

How to make **Creamed Cakes**

Some of the most traditional cakes, such as chocolate cake, are creamed cakes, which simply means you beat together the sugar and butter to a soft, creamy consistency before adding the other ingredients. Creaming is important because it gets air into the mixture to create perfectly light and fluffy cakes every time.

Using an electric hand mixer is far easier than beating with a wooden spoon by hand and gets far more air into the mix

Hold the edge of the bowl steady while beating

Always make sure you use softened butter for easy and thorough creaming

Creaming

Beat the butter and sugar together until the mixture is light and fluffy. Using an electric hand mixer is far easier than beating with a wooden spoon by hand and gets far more air into the mix. Creaming cuts the sugar crystals into the butter, creating air pockets, and so the more thoroughly you cream the mix, the lighter the cake will be.

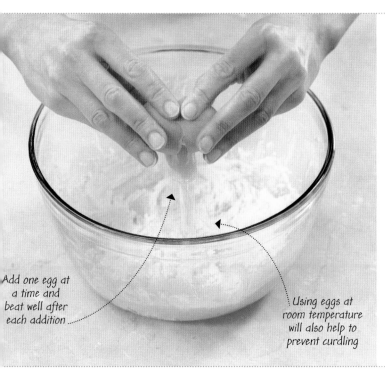

Add one egg at a time and beat well after each addition

Using eggs at room temperature will also help to prevent curdling

Adding the eggs

Eggs are added to the butter and sugar mixture to bind all the ingredients together—they act as an emulsifier blending the ingredients for a smoother texture. Make sure to add the eggs gradually, since adding the eggs too quickly can curdle the mix and make it look like scrambled eggs. Do not panic if that happens— simply add a tablespoon of flour with each addition of egg, then stir in the remaining flour.

Sifting and folding

The dry ingredients are sifted together to help separate and aerate the flour particles, making them absorb liquids better and adding volume to the cake. To avoid knocking any of the air out, fold in the dry ingredients gently with a large metal spoon.

The science of Baking Cakes

Baking a cake harnesses precise chemical processes to transform a few simple ingredients into a mouth-watering slice of magic. Knowing the science involved in these transformations will help you to understand why certain ingredients and particular techniques create the best results.

1 Vigorously beating together fat and sugar—or "creaming"—creates an airy foam. As the ingredients are beaten, bubbles of air fix to the rough edges of the sugar crystals and are held in place by a film of fat.

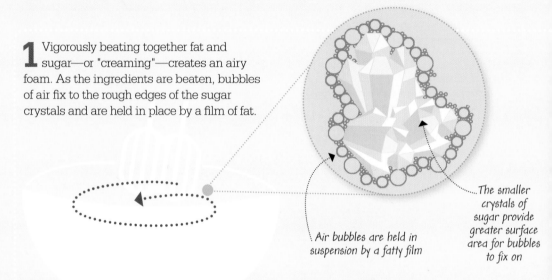

Air bubbles are held in suspension by a fatty film

The smaller crystals of sugar provide greater surface area for bubbles to fix on

2 In the heat of the oven, as the air in the foam expands and the fat melts, the bubbles would burst. To prevent this, eggs are also beaten in, which, under heat, solidify around the bubbles to keep them intact.

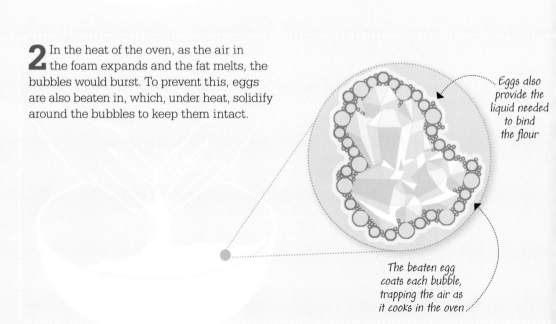

Eggs also provide the liquid needed to bind the flour

The beaten egg coats each bubble, trapping the air as it cooks in the oven

3 When mixed with a liquid, proteins in flour bind together to form a network of glutens, which soldify in the oven and provide structure to the cake. If too many glutens form, however, the cake will have a tough rather than soft and crumbly texture.

Gluten forms when two different proteins in flour bind together in long strands

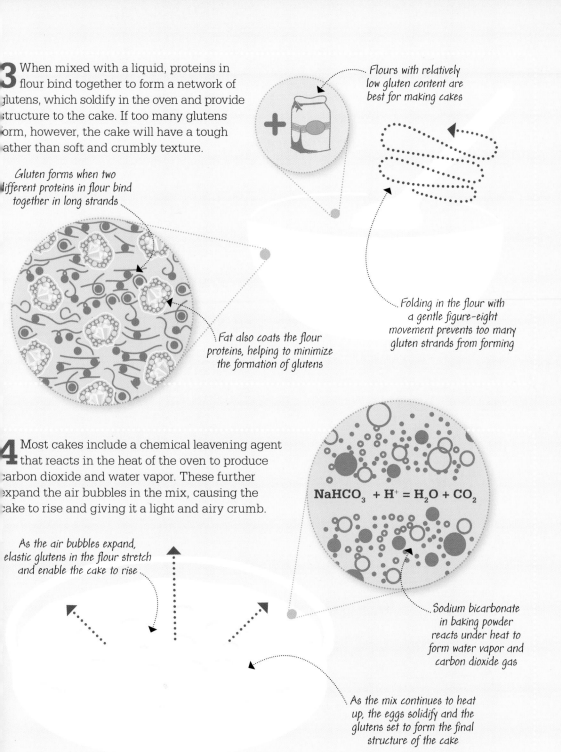

Flours with relatively low gluten content are best for making cakes

Folding in the flour with a gentle figure-eight movement prevents too many gluten strands from forming

Fat also coats the flour proteins, helping to minimize the formation of glutens

4 Most cakes include a chemical leavening agent that reacts in the heat of the oven to produce carbon dioxide and water vapor. These further expand the air bubbles in the mix, causing the cake to rise and giving it a light and airy crumb.

$$NaHCO_3 + H^+ = H_2O + CO_2$$

As the air bubbles expand, elastic glutens in the flour stretch and enable the cake to rise

Sodium bicarbonate in baking powder reacts under heat to form water vapor and carbon dioxide gas

As the mix continues to heat up, the eggs solidify and the glutens set to form the final structure of the cake

Chocolate Cake

The secret to a good creamed cake is quite simply air and
more air, since this will guarantee a light and fluffy cake.
Try this classic chocolate cake, with a filling of
buttercream and a sprinkling of sugar, to prove to
yourself just how easy it is to make a creamed cake.

Serves 6–8

Bakes in 20–25 minutes

Up to 8 weeks, unfilled

ngredients

tbsp unsalted butter, softened, plus extra for greasing

cup light brown sugar

large eggs

cup self-rising flour

cup cocoa powder

tsp baking powder

tbsp Greek yogurt or thick plain yogurt

or the chocolate buttercream

tbsp unsalted butter, softened

cup confectioners' sugar, plus extra for dusting

cup cocoa powder

little milk, if needed

pecial equipment

x 7in (18cm) round cake pans

unsalted butter **light brown sugar** **eggs**

self-rising flour **cocoa powder** **baking powder**

yogurt **confectioners' sugar** **round cake pans**

Total time *55–60 minutes*

Prepare
5 minutes

Make
25 minutes

Bake
20–25 minutes

Decorate
5 minutes

1 Preheat the oven to 350°F (180°C). Grease the cake pans with butter. Line the bottom and sides with parchment. Set aside.

Tip For the sides, cut a length just longer than the pan's circumference. Make short 45° cuts with scissors along one of the long edges; this will then fold and sit neatly on the bottom. For the bottom, place a pan on parchment paper, draw a circle around the pan, and cut it out.

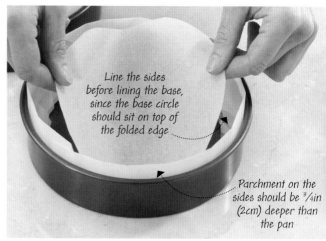

Line the sides before lining the base, since the base circle should sit on top of the folded edge

Parchment on the sides should be ¾in (2cm) deeper than the pan

Scrape down the sides of the bowl with a spatula to mix evenly

2 Place the softened butter and sugar in a large mixing bowl. Use a hand mixer to cream the two ingredients together until light and fluffy.

Remember You must cream the butter and sugar together for at least 2–3 minutes, otherwise your cake won't have a light texture. The more you beat at this stage, the more air you get into the mixture.

3 Add the eggs one at a time to the creamed mixture, beating well after each addition using an electric whisk. To begin with, the eggs will seem separate from the creamed mix, but with enough blending, they will eventually combine and take on an "emulsified" or a well-blended appearance that is soft and creamy-looking.

The creamed mixture should look light and fluffy

4 Sift the flour, cocoa, and baking powder into a separate bowl. Then, with a metal spoon, gently fold into the mixture using a figure-eight motion. Also fold in the yogurt. The flour mixture must be gently folded in to avoid knocking any of the all-important air out of the mixture.

Tip Though not essential, for a really well aerated mix, you can sift the dry ingredients a second time.

Hold the sieve as high as you dare ....

Gently tap the edge of the sieve

Spread the mixture right into the edges of the pan .

5 Divide the mixture evenly between the 2 cake pans by placing alternate spoonfuls of the mix into each pan until you have the same amount in both the pans. Then smooth the mixture with a palette knife and bake for 20–25 minutes until well risen.

Tip Spread the mixture out so that there is a slight hollow in the center, to prevent the cake from peaking in the center.

6 The cakes are cooked when a skewer inserted into their centers comes out clean (see p.19, step 6). Let cool in their pans for 5 minutes, then remove from the pans and move the cakes to a wire rack to cool completely. Remove the parchment paper.

Help! Don't panic if the skewer comes out with some cake mixture on it. Simply bake the cakes for a few more minutes and then retest.

Peel off the parchment only after the cake cools down— any earlier and you may pull out some of the cake .

7 To make the buttercream filling, mix together the butter, confectioners' sugar, and cocoa by beating them together quite vigorously until smooth, soft, and thoroughly blended.

Help! If the buttercream is a little firm, add a drop of milk to the mixture and mix again until it is soft enough to spread.

After mixing, the buttercream should be soft enough to spread

Use a palette knife to spread the buttercream

8 Turn one cake flat-side up and spread with the buttercream. Top with the other cake, keeping the flat sides together. Transfer to a serving plate. Sift a little confectioners' sugar evenly over the top by holding the sieve above the cake and tapping very gently, moving the sieve across the cake for even coverage.

Tip This cake will keep for 2 days if stored in an airtight container.

The perfect **Chocolate Cake**

The perfect chocolate cake will be deliciously light and fluffy in texture with moist but well-risen layers when baked.

Top of the cake has a light dusting of sugar

Layer of buttercream is thick and spread out evenly

Cake has a light and airy texture

Did anything go wrong?

The cake has sunk in the middle. You may have taken it out of the oven before it was cooked through. Next time, test your cake using a metal skewer and don't open the oven door too early to prevent the cake from sinking.

The cake has a heavy texture. You may have added the eggs too quickly, which caused the mixture to curdle. A curdled cake mix will not bake well because the mixture will be lumpy and separated, resulting in a coarser and heavier cake.

The cake seems too dry. You may have overcooked the cake or left it out for too long once cooled.

The cake has risen too much in the center. You may have set the oven temperature to too high or added too much baking powder.

The cake hasn't risen very well. You may have either used insufficient baking powder or may have overbeaten the mixture, knocking the air out.

The sides of the cake are wet. You may not have removed the cake early enough from the pans to cool properly.

Try more Creamed Cake recipes ▶ ▶ ▶

Victoria Sponge Cake

Serves 6–8

Bakes in 20–25 minutes

Up to 4 weeks, unfilled

Ingredients

1 stick, plus 4 tbsp unsalted butter, softened, plus extra for greasing

¾ cup sugar

3 large eggs, at room temperature

1 tsp pure vanilla extract

1¼ cups self-rising flour

1 tsp baking powder

For the filling

4 tbsp unsalted butter, softened

⅓ cup confectioners' sugar, plus extra for dusting

1 tsp pure vanilla extract

⅓ cup good-quality seedless raspberry jam

Special Equipment

2 x 7in (18cm) round cake pans

Preheat the oven to 350°F (180°C). Grease the pans and line the bottom and sides with parchment paper. Set aside.

PREPARE THE MIXTURE

Cream together the butter and sugar using a hand mixer until light and fluffy. Add the eggs one at a time, beating well after each addition.

Careful! Always make sure the eggs are at room temperature to help prevent curdling.

Add the vanilla and blend into the creamed mixture. Then beat for another 2 minutes or until bubbles appear on the surface. Remove the beaters then sift together the flour and baking powder into the bowl. With a metal spoon, gently fold the flour into the mixture using a figure-eight motion.

BAKE THE CAKE

Divide the mixture between the pans and smooth the tops with a palette knife. Bake for 20–25 minutes until well risen. The cakes are cooked when a metal skewer inserted into their centers comes out clean.

Help! Don't panic if the skewer has cake mixture on it. Simply bake for a few more minutes and retest.

Let the cakes cool in the pans for 5 minutes, then remove the parchment paper and move the cakes to a wire rack to cool completely.

DECORATE AND SERVE

To make the buttercream filling, beat together the butter, confectioners' sugar, and vanilla until smooth and well mixed. Transfer one cake to a serving plate, flat side up. Spread with buttercream.

Tip If the buttercream is a little firm, add a drop of milk to thin it slightly.

Spread the jam on top of the buttercream. Place the other cake on top of the filling, keeping the flat sides together. Sieve a generous layer of confectioners' sugar over the cake and serve in slices.

Coffee and Walnut Cake

Serves 8 | **Bakes in 20–25 minutes** | **8 weeks, unfilled**

Ingredients

2 sticks, plus 3 tbsp unsalted butter, softened, plus extra for greasing

1 cup light brown sugar

3 large eggs, at room temperature

1 tsp pure vanilla extract

1¼ cups self-rising flour

1 tsp baking powder

1 tbsp strong coffee powder mixed with 2 tbsp boiling water and cooled, or equivalent espresso

1 cup confectioners' sugar, sifted

9 walnut halves

Special Equipment

2 x 7in (18cm) round cake pans

Preheat the oven to 350°F (180°C). Grease and line the cake pans with parchment paper.

PREPARE THE MIXTURE

Place 12 tbsp of the butter and the sugar in a large bowl and, using a hand mixer, cream together for 2–3 minutes or until light and fluffy. Add the eggs to the creamed mixture one at a time, beating well after each addition to prevent curdling.

Remember Using eggs at room temperature reduces the risk of curdling.

Stir in the vanilla. Sift the flour and baking powder, and fold into the creamed mixture until well mixed. Stir in half of the coffee mixture and make sure it is well incorporated.

BAKE THE CAKE

Divide the mixture between the 2 pans and smooth over their surfaces using a palette knife. Bake in the oven for 20–25 minutes or until well risen and a metal skewer comes out clean.

Remember Another way to check if the cakes are cooked is to see if they have begun to shrink away from the sides of their pans.

Leave the cakes in their pans for 5 minutes to cool slightly. Then remove from the tins and move to wire racks, discarding the parchment paper, to cool completely.

FILL, DECORATE, AND SERVE

To make the buttercream, place the remaining butter and confectioners' sugar in a bowl and beat with a hand mixer until very smooth. Then beat in the remaining coffee mixture. Using a palette knife, evenly spread the flat side of one cake with half of the buttercream. Top with the other cake and spread with the remaining buttercream. Move to a serving plate, decorate with walnuts, slice, and serve.

Toffee Apple Cake

Serves 8–10

Bakes in 40–45 minutes

Up to 4 weeks

Ingredients

1 stick, plus 6 tbsp unsalted butter, softened, plus extra for greasing

¼ cup sugar

1⅔ cups (9oz) peeled, cubed apples (1 large apple)

1⅔ cups light brown sugar

3 large eggs

1 cup self-rising flour

1 heaping tsp baking powder

whipped cream, to serve (optional)

Special Equipment

9in (23cm) round springform cake pan

Preheat the oven to 350°F (180°C). Grease the cake pan and line its bottom with parchment paper.

PREPARE THE MIXTURE

In a frying pan, heat 3 tablespoons of the butter. Add the sugar and heat until melted and golden brown. Stir in the cubed apple and fry gently for 7–8 minutes, until they just start to soften and caramelize.

Careful! Constantly stir the apple mixture while cooking to prevent it from sticking.

Place the remaining butter and sugar in a large bowl and, using a hand mixer, cream together for 2–3 minutes or until light and fluffy. Add the eggs to the creamed mixture one at a time and beat well after each addition to prevent curdling. Sift together the flour and baking powder, then gently fold into the creamed mixture until well mixed. Using a slotted spoon, remove the apple from the pan, reserving the syrup, and scatter the apple over the bottom of the cake pan. Spoon the mixture on top, smooth over the surface with a palette knife, and place on a baking sheet to catch any drips.

BAKE AND FINISH

Bake in the preheated oven for 40–45 minutes or until well risen and a metal skewer comes out clean. Leave the cake to cool in the pan for at least 5 minutes, then carefully remove it from the pan, flipping it over so the apples are on top, and discarding the paper. Let cool slightly on a wire rack. Gently heat the reserved apple syrup until warmed through and runny.

Why? You will need to reheat the reserved apple syrup, since it may have thickened too much to be of a pourable consistency.

Make holes over the surface of the cake, using a fine skewer, and transfer the cake to a serving plate. Pour the apple syrup over the top of the cake and allow time for it to soak into the holes. Serve the cake in slices while still warm, with whipped cream, if liked.

Cherry and Almond Cake

Serves 8–10 | **Bakes in 1½–1¾ hours** | **Up to 4 weeks**

Ingredients

stick, plus 3 tbsp unsalted butter, softened, plus extra for greasing

14oz (400g) pitted cherries

⅔ cup sugar

2 large eggs at room temperature

1¾ cups self-rising flour, sifted

1 tsp baking powder

5oz (150g) ground almonds

1 tsp pure vanilla extract

½ cup whole milk

¼ cup (scant 1oz) whole blanched almonds, halved

Special Equipment

8in (20cm) round springform cake pan

cherry pitter (optional)

Preheat the oven to 350°F (180°C). Grease the cake pan and line the bottom with parchment paper. Remove the cherry pits with a cherry pitter. Alternatively, take a toothpick and push it into the cherry where the stem was, and as soon as it hits the pit, twist the toothpick around and pull the cherry pit out.

PREPARE THE MIXTURE

Place the butter and sugar in a large bowl and, using a hand mixer, cream together for 2–3 minutes, or until light and fluffy. Add the eggs to the creamed mixture, one at a time, with a tablespoon of flour and beat well after each addition.

Why? Adding a tablespoon of flour with each egg prevents the cake mixture from curdling.

Mix in the remaining flour, baking powder, ground almonds, vanilla, and milk. Add half the cherries, then spoon the mixture into the pan, smoothing over the surface. Scatter the remaining cherries and almonds on the top.

BAKE THE CAKE

Bake in the preheated oven for 1½–1¾ hours or until golden brown and firm to the touch.

Careful! If the cake begins to brown too much, simply cover the top with foil.

Check if the cake is cooked through by inserting a metal skewer into the center of the cake. If it comes out clean, the cake is cooked; if not, cook for a few minutes longer and retest. Remove the cake from the oven and let it cool in the pan for at least 15 minutes. Then carefully remove the cake from the pan, discarding the paper, and transfer to a wire rack to cool completely. Slice and serve.

Tip This cake will keep for up to 2 days if stored in an airtight container.

How to make **Brownies**

Brownies are a cross between a cake and a cookie and are typically
made with melted chocolate and sometimes nuts for extra crunch.
For the perfectly rich and chewy brownie, it's essential that you melt
the chocolate and butter slowly. And, whatever you do, don't overbake
your brownies, or they will lose their delicious, moist texture.

Careful! It is important that the bottom of the bowl sits above the water and doesn't touch it, or the chocolate will overheat and become grainy.

Don't forget to scrape the sides of the bowl

Melting the butter and chocolate

Begin by slowly melting the chocolate and
butter in a bowl over a pan of simmering
water. Never heat the chocolate in a pan
over direct heat, since this will cause the
chocolate to overheat and turn grainy, or,
worse still, "seize," which means it suddenly
turns into an irreversible solid, grainy mass.

Also make sure that the mixture doesn't
come into contact with the water, since this
could also cause the chocolate to seize.
Stirring constantly with a wooden spoon
keeps the temperature of the mixture even,
prevents the chocolate from overheating, and
helps to combine the butter and chocolate.

The mixture will thicken considerably on adding the eggs

Using eggs at room temperature will help prevent the mixture from curdling

Adding the eggs

Eggs form the next element in a brownie batter. Let the chocolate mixture cool before adding the beaten eggs, or the eggs will start cooking when you add them. To make a smooth batter, add the eggs slowly, a little at a time, stirring after each addition.

Gently tap the side of the sieve

Sieving the cocoa and flour together helps to mix them

Adding the flour

The final element of a basic brownie batter is flour, sometimes combined with cocoa. To add extra air, sift these dry ingredients into the chocolate mixture, and then gently fold them in with a spatula, using a figure-eight motion. This avoids knocking any air out, which would deflate the batter and result in heavy brownies.

The flour and cocoa particles attract air as they fall

Chocolate and Hazelnut Brownies

To achieve the perfect brownie, one that is rich, moist, and
chewy, you need to follow just a few simple rules. Try this
chocolate and hazelnut brownie recipe—great for an
entry into the world of brownie-making.

akes 24 | **Bakes in 12–15 minutes** | **Unsuitable for freezing**

gredients

up hazelnuts

z (300g) good-quality dark chocolate, roken into pieces

tbsp unsalted butter, cubed

cups sugar

arge eggs, beaten

cups all-purpose flour

cup cocoa powder, plus extra for dusting

pecial Equipment

13in (23 x 32cm) rectangular rownie pan, or similar

hazelnuts

dark chocolate

unsalted butter

sugar

beaten eggs

all-purpose flour

cocoa powder

rectangular brownie pan

Total time *47–50 minutes, plus cooling*

Prepare
5 minutes

Make
25 minutes

Bake
12–15 minutes

Decorate
5 minutes

1 Preheat the oven to 400°F (200°C). Scatter the hazelnuts on a baking sheet and toast in the oven for 5 minutes. Rub them in a dish towel to remove their skins, then transfer to a cutting board, and coarsely chop using a large knife. Set aside.

Tip For an interesting texture, chop some of the hazelnuts into big chunks and some into small.

Toasting the hazelnuts makes it easier to rub their skins off, but be careful not to burn them

Make sure the bowl is supported by the pan and not sitting in the water, otherwise the chocolate will overheat

2 Put the chopped chocolate and butter in a heatproof bowl and place it over a pan of simmering water. Heat until melted and smooth, stirring occasionally. Cool slightly for 5 minutes, then stir in the sugar until well mixed.

Careful! Do not let the water heat above simmering point, since this could cause the chocolate to become grainy.

3 Add the eggs a little at a time, mixing well between each addition, until you have a smooth mixture.

Careful! Before adding the eggs, make sure they are at room temperature and the chocolate mixture has cooled down sufficiently, or you'll end up with scrambled eggs.

Use a wooden spoon to beat the mixture very vigorously

4 Sift the flour and cocoa into the mixture, holding the sieve at a height to incorporate as much air as possible. Gently fold in the flour and cocoa until everything is fully mixed in. Add the chopped roasted hazelnuts into the batter and fold in until the nuts are mixed and evenly distributed.

Tip For best results, sift the flour and cocoa together twice, using a separate bowl, before folding in.

Add the hazelnuts when no traces of flour or cocoa are left

For ease of spreading, use a spatula

5 Line the brownie pan with parchment paper, then add the batter. Using a spatula, spread the mixture out evenly so that it fills the corners properly, and smooth over the top.

Tip Leave a little extra parchment paper around the sides of the pan for easy removal.

Make diagonal cuts into the corners of the parchment so it fits easily into the corners of the pan

Try to get the surface as smooth and even as possible

6 Bake the brownies in the oven for 12–15 minutes. Test if they have baked on top by pressing the middle with two fingers: it should feel firm to the touch. Test that the centers are still chewy by inserting a skewer.

Remember Brownies should be chewy, and it's best to underbake them, since they firm up once cooled. Check them after 10–12 minutes of baking.

...The brownies are dor if a skewer inserted comes out coated with a little batter, but not a lot of very wet batter

7 Leave the brownies to cool down completely in the pan. This helps to maintain their soft, chewy center and, being very fragile at this stage, they could break if removed from the pan any sooner. When cool, carefully lift them from the pan and place then on a cutting board.

Tip Use the edges of the baking parchment paper to help lift the brownies out of the pan.

8 Put freshly boiled water in a shallow bowl. Using a knife, cut the brownies into 24 squares, dipping the knife in the hot water as you go. Place 1 tablespoon of cocoa in a sieve, hold it over the brownies, and gently tap with your hand to give the brownies a light coating of cocoa. Then serve.

Why? Wetting the knife helps you to cut the brownies cleanly without the mix sticking to the knife.

...You can cut the brownies into larger squares, if preferred

The perfect **Chocolate and Hazelnut Brownies**

Your cooked brownies should be firm around the edge, but their centers should be deliciously soft and chewy.

A flat surface

Cut into even squares

A generous layer of cocoa on top

An even distribution of chopped nuts

Did anything go wrong?

The brownie batter looks lumpy and curdled.
You may have added the eggs before the chocolate mixture had cooled down enough or used eggs that were straight from the fridge and too cold.

The brownies are far too wet. You may not have baked them for long enough or you used a pan that was smaller than the one suggested. If the pan is a bit smaller, the brownie mix will be more compacted. Increase the cooking time by a minute or two, checking frequently to see if it is cooked.

The brownies collapsed when removed from the pan. You may not have cooled the brownies completely before removing them from the pan. Remember, they firm up a lot when completely cooled.

The brownies are very dry. You may have baked them for too long. It's important to get the texture right, so if in doubt, underbake them.

The brownies are tough. The batter may have been overbeaten after adding the eggs and flour. Gently fold these in so as not to knock the air out.

The brownies are heavy. The batter may have been overbeaten after folding in the flour and cocoa.

Some of the brownies have more nuts than the others. You may not have stirred the nuts into the batter evenly.

Try more Brownie recipes ▶ ▶ ▶

Sour Cherry and Chocolate Brownies

Makes 16

Bakes in 20–25 minutes

Unsuitable for freezing

Ingredients

11 tbsp unsalted butter, cubed
plus extra for greasing

6oz (150g) good-quality dark chocolate,
broken into pieces

1¼ cups light brown sugar

3 eggs, lightly beaten

1 tsp pure vanilla extract

1¼ cups self-rising flour

½ cup dried sour cherries

4oz (100g) dark chocolate chunks

Special Equipment

8 x 10in (20 x 25cm) brownie pan, or similar-sized
deep baking sheet

Preheat the oven to 350°F (180°C). Grease
the pan and line with parchment paper.

PREPARE THE MIXTURE

Place the butter and chocolate in a heatproof
bowl and sit the bowl over a saucepan of
simmering water, stirring occasionally, until
melted and smooth (see p.96). Remove from
the heat and stir in the sugar, then cool slightly
for 5 minutes. Mix the eggs and vanilla extract
into the cooled chocolate mixture.

Careful! Let your chocolate mixture cool slightly
before adding the eggs, otherwise they will
begin to cook.

Sift the flour into a bowl, then pour the chocolate
mixture onto the flour and stir until just well
combined, taking care not to overwork the mixture.
Then fold in the cherries and chocolate chunks.

BAKE THE BROWNIES

Pour the mixture into the prepared pan and
spread it out to the corners, smoothing the
mixture over so it's even. Bake for 20–25 minutes.
The brownie is ready when the edges are firm
but the middle is still soft. Let cool in the
pan, since it will be very fragile, before carefully
turning out and cutting into 16 squares.

Remember Brownies are supposed to be slightly
soft in the center after baking so, unlike other
cakes, if testing with a skewer, it should not
come out clean.

Tip These brownies will keep very well for up
to 3 days if stored in an airtight container.

White Chocolate and Macadamia Blondies

Makes 24

Bakes in 20 minutes

Unsuitable for freezing

Ingredients

10oz (300g) white chocolate, broken
    into pieces

12 tbsp unsalted butter, cubed

1⅓ cups sugar

4 large eggs

1⅔ cups all-purpose flour

1 cup macadamia nuts,
    coarsely chopped

Special Equipment

8 x 10in (20 x 25cm) brownie pan, or similar-sized
    deep baking sheet

Preheat the oven to 400°F (200°C). Grease
the pan and line with parchment paper.

PREPARE THE MIXTURE

Place the chocolate and butter in a heatproof
bowl and sit the bowl over a saucepan of
simmering water, stirring occasionally, until
melted and smooth (see p.96). Do not let the
bowl touch the water.

Careful! The mixture must be melted over just
simmering, and not boiling, water, otherwise the
chocolate will overheat and become grainy.

Remove the bowl from the heat, stir in the
sugar, and cool for 10 minutes before adding the
eggs. Beat the eggs into the melted mixture one
at a time, making sure each one is well mixed in
before adding the next. Sift in the flour, add the
nuts, and stir together until just mixed.

BAKE THE BLONDIES

Pour the mixture into the prepared pan and
gently spread it out to the corners. Bake for
20 minutes or until just firm to the touch on top
but still soft underneath.

Remember The blondies will firm up more
on cooling.

Remove from the oven and let cool completely
in the pan, since the blondies will be very fragile.
Then cut into 24 squares or 12 rectangles.

Tip These blondies will keep very well for up
to 5 days if stored in an airtight container.

How to make **Baked Cheesecake**

Baked cheesecakes typically have a crushed cookie base and a creamy, velvety-smooth topping. Unlike the cheesecakes that are set with gelatin, they rely on the eggs in the mix to set the filling during baking. Sometimes flour is included in the cream cheese mix to bind the ingredients, as well as cream and different cream cheeses, such as ricotta or mascarpone.

Roll across the bag until the cookies resemble fine bread crumbs

Expel excess air

Crushing the cookies

To make the base, first put the cookies in a freezer bag. Seal and roll a rolling pin across the bag until the crumbs are of a uniform size. A fine crumb will hold the cheesecake's base together whereas a coarse crumb will crumble and fall apart more easily. You can also crush the cookies in a food processor.

Making the cookie base

Mixing butter into the cookie crumbs binds the crumbs together to give the cheesecake a firm base. To form the base, press the mixture firmly into the cake pan, or other dish, using the back of a spoon.

Make sure the cookie mixture completely covers the bottom of the pan, otherwise the filling will escape

Blending the filling

Blend the filling ingredients thoroughly so you don't get a lumpy mix. It also helps if your cream cheese and eggs are at room temperature before you beat them together. The eggs act as an emulsifier, binding together the ingredients that normally wouldn't mix easily. If using a food processor, stop as soon as the mix is fully blended, so you don't get too many air bubbles in the mix, which could cause the surface to crack during baking.

You can blend the filling ingredients by hand, but it's quicker and more thorough to use a food processor

The cheesecake is ready if it feels slightly wobbly in the center

Why? Cheesecakes are often baked in a bath of boiling water. This insulates the pan from direct heat and maintains a low cooking temperature, allowing the cheesecake to cook slowly and evenly.

Testing for a set

The key to a perfect cheesecake is knowing when to stop baking it. If cooked perfectly, the edges will be set but the center will still be wobbly, since the filling will firm up more as it cools. If you overbake the cheesecake it will become tough and rubbery in texture.

Practice BAKED CHEESECAKE

Blueberry Ripple Cheesecake

The ripple effect of this cheesecake looks impressive and is guaranteed to deliver the "wow" factor when entertaining friends or family. However, don't be put off by this, since it's surprisingly simple to achieve.

erves 8

Bakes in 40 minutes, plus cooling

Unsuitable for freezing

unsalted butter

vanilla wafers

blueberries

gredients

bsp unsalted butter, plus
extra for greasing

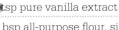

z (125g) vanilla wafers

z (150g) blueberries

cup sugar, plus
3 tbsp extra

bz (400g) cream cheese,
at room temperature

z (250g) mascarpone,
at room temperature

arge eggs, plus 1 large egg yolk,
at room temperature

tsp pure vanilla extract

bsp all-purpose flour, sifted

sugar

cream cheese

mascarpone

eggs

vanilla
extract

all-purpose
flour

egg yolk

pecial Equipment

n (20cm) deep springform cake pan

od processor with blade attachment

springform cake pan

food processor

Total time *1 hour 5 minutes, plus at least 5 hours cooling and chilling*

Prep
5 minutes

Make
20 minutes

Bake
40 minutes

1 Preheat the oven to 350°F (180°C) and grease the cake pan well with butter. Crush the cookies in a freezer bag using a rolling pin. Melt the butter in a pan and stir in the cookie crumbs. Spoon the mixture into the pan, pressing it down firmly and evenly.

Tip Heat the butter over low heat to keep from burning it, since this would give a burned flavor and an unwanted brown color.

...To avoid a crumbly base ensure the crumbs are well coated in butter

2 Process the blueberries and 3 tbsp of sugar in a food processor until smooth. Sieve the purée to remove the skins, place it in a pan, and boil for 3–5 minutes to achieve a jamlike consistency, so that it can be marbled into the cheese mix without sinking. Once thickened, set aside.

Why? Boiling the purée vigorously helps concentrate the flavor and also gives it a jamlike consistency.

3 In a food processor, blend the remaining sugar, cream cheese, mascarpone, eggs, vanilla extract, and flour. Stop processing once thoroughly blended and smooth, or you'll add air bubbles, which will cause the cheesecake to crack when baked. Spoon the mix into the pan and smooth the surface with a spatula.

Remember Make sure your cheeses are soft before blending.

Check the mixture properly mixed, wr no traces of egg, cream cheese, or flour

Don't forget to scrape down the sides of the processor bowl

4 Drizzle on the blueberry mix and swirl it using a skewer. Wrap the base and sides of the pan with foil and place in a roasting pan half-filled with boiling water. Bake for 40 minutes, until set but wobbly in the center. Turn off the oven. Leave for 1 hour, then remove from the oven and cool completely on a wire rack. Transfer to the refrigerator to chill for at least 4 hours or overnight.

lace dollops of the blueberry mix evenly over the filling, then break them up with a skewer, making swirls

The perfect **Blueberry Ripple Cheesecake**

For a blueberry compote to serve alongside the cheesecake, gently heat 4oz (100g) blueberries with 1 tablespoon of sugar and a squeeze of lemon juice in a small pan until the sugar dissolves and the berries start to release their juices.

Did anything go wrong?

The cheesecake mixture is lumpy. You may not have mixed the ingredients well or they were probably not at room temperature before mixing.

The cheesecake has sunk in the center. Did you let it cool slowly in the turned-off oven before chilling?

The cheesecake split open when it was removed from the pan. You need to grease the pan well before adding the filling and run a palette knife around the edges to free the cheesecake before serving.

The cheesecake has a rubbery texture. You may have overbaked the cheesecake. Next time check earlier to see if it has baked. Don't be put off by a wobbly center—it should be just firm to the touch in the center and still a little wobbly. If it is not, it is overbaked, and if a finger pressed in the middle leaves a dent, it is underbaked.

The surface is smooth and not cracked

The base is crunchy

The cheese filling is smooth and set, and firmer around the edge

Try more Baked Cheesecake recipes ▶ ▶ ▶

Chocolate Marble Cheesecake

Serves 8–10 | **Bakes in 60 minutes, plus cooling** | **Unsuitable for freezing**

Ingredients

5 tbsp unsalted butter, melted, plus extra for greasing

6oz (150g) vanilla wafers, finely crushed

6oz (150g) good-quality dark chocolate, broken into pieces

1lb 2oz (500g) cream cheese, softened

⅔ cup sugar

1 tsp pure vanilla extract

2 large eggs, at room temperature

Special Equipment

8in (20cm) round springform cake pan

Grease the cake pan with butter and chill.

MAKE THE BASE AND FILLING

Add the melted butter to the cookie crumbs, stirring until well mixed, then spoon into the pan and press the mixture over the base and up the sides of the pan. Chill for 30–60 minutes or until firm. Preheat the oven to 350°F (180°C). Place the chocolate in a heatproof bowl set over a pan of simmering water and heat until melted and smooth (see p.96). Remove from the heat and allow to cool slightly.

Careful! Make sure the water is just simmering, since too much heat will cause the chocolate to turn grainy.

Beat the cream cheese in a bowl until smooth. Add the sugar and vanilla and beat well. Add the eggs, one at a time, beating well after each addition. Pour half of this mixture into the lined pan. Stir the melted and cooled chocolate into the remaining half of the cheesecake mixture. Spoon a ring of the chocolate filling over the plain filling and, using a metal skewer, swirl the fillings together to create an attractive marbled effect.

BAKE AND SERVE

Bake the cheesecake for 50–60 minutes, at which point most of the cheesecake is firm, but the center will still wobble slightly. Turn off the oven and leave the cheesecake inside to cool for 1½ hours.

Why? Cooling down the cheesecake in the turned-off oven helps prevent it from cracking.

Remove the cooled cheesecake from the oven and chill in the fridge for at least 4 hours, or ideally overnight. To serve, run a knife around the side of the pan to loosen it, remove from the pan, and arrange on a serving plate. Serve in slices.

Tip The cheesecake can be made up to 3 days ahead and stored wrapped in plastic wrap in the fridge until needed.

Ginger Cheesecake

Serves 8–10 | **Bakes in 60 minutes, plus cooling** | **Unsuitable for freezing**

Ingredients

5 tbsp unsalted butter, melted, plus extra for greasing

5oz (150g) vanilla wafers, finely crushed

1lb 2oz (500g) cream cheese, softened

5oz (125g) pieces of preserved ginger in syrup, chopped, plus 3 tbsp syrup

finely grated zest of 1 lemon

2 tsp lemon juice

1 cup sour cream

⅓ cup sugar

1 tsp pure vanilla extract

4 large eggs, at room temperature

⅓ cup heavy cream, to top (optional)

Special Equipment

8in (20cm) round springform cake pan

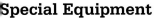

Grease the cake pan with butter and chill.

MAKE THE BASE AND FILLING

Add the melted butter to the biscuit crumbs, stirring until well mixed, then spoon into the pan and press the mixture over the base and up the sides of the pan. Chill for 30–60 minutes or until firm. Preheat the oven to 180°C (350°F/Gas 4). Beat the cream cheese in a bowl until smooth.

Careful! Always ensure your cream cheese is very smooth before beating in the other ingredients, otherwise you will have a lumpy filling.

Add the chopped ginger (reserving 2 tablespoons to decorate), ginger syrup, lemon zest and juice, sour cream, sugar, and vanilla. Beat until smooth.

Add the eggs one at a time, beating well after each addition. Pour the filling onto the base and shake slightly to level the surface.

BAKE AND DECORATE

Place the pan on a baking tray and bake in the oven for 50–60 minutes. The cheesecake is cooked when most of it is firm, but the center will still wobble slightly. Turn off the oven and leave the cheesecake inside to cool for 1½ hours.

Why? Cooling down the cheesecake in the turned-off oven helps prevent it from cracking.

Chill in the fridge for 4 hours, or ideally overnight. If using double cream, whip it until it forms soft peaks. To serve, run a knife around the side of the pan to loosen it. Remove from the pan and arrange on a serving plate. Swirl or smooth the cream over the top of the cheesecake and decorate with a scattering of the reserved chopped stem ginger. Serve in slices.

Tip The cheesecake can be made up to 3 days in advance and stored wrapped in plastic wrap in the fridge.

How to make **Pie Dough**

Pie dough is one of the easiest pastries to make. It is used when making savory and sweet tarts and pies, and it doesn't puff up on baking. For light and meltingly tender pie dough, the key is to keep everything cold, including your hands, and not to overwork the dough.

Lift the flour with pieces of the butter, keeping the palms facing up to aerate the mix, and rub between your thumb and fingers to form fine crumbs

Hands are cool

Butter is cool, straight from the fridge

Sift the flour first to add extra air and lightness to the dough

Tip To save time, you can pulse the flour and butter together in a food processor until the mixture resembles fine bread crumbs.

Rubbing in

This technique coats the flour with the butter, reducing gluten formation when mixing the dough. This gives a tenderness to the finished pie dough. It is important to use only your fingertips when rubbing the butter into the flour, since this minimizes contact with body heat, which will melt the butter and make the dough heavy and greasy.

Always use cold water to bind the dough, since warm water will make the dough greasy

Shape the dough into a rough ball as soon as it holds together

As soon as the mixture holds together, stop mixing, or you will overwork the dough, making it tough

Forming the dough

Begin by mixing in enough cold water to bind the dough together. Use a round-bladed knife until the mixture begins to come together to form a soft, but not sticky, dough. Too much water will cause the dough to steam on baking, which will make it flimsy and shrink back. Sometimes egg yolk is also added, which may be enough to bind the dough together without any additional, or very little, water. Then form into a rough ball with your hands.

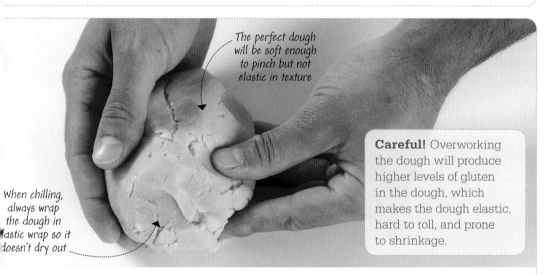

The perfect dough will be soft enough to pinch but not elastic in texture

When chilling, always wrap the dough in plastic wrap so it doesn't dry out

Careful! Overworking the dough will produce higher levels of gluten in the dough, which makes the dough elastic, hard to roll, and prone to shrinkage.

Shaping and relaxing

Pie dough must be chilled in the fridge for at least 30 minutes to relax the gluten in the dough and to prevent it from shrinking back as it bakes. Shape it into a ball without overworking the dough, which can make it greasy and tough.

The science of Making Pie Dough

Pie dough should remain fundamentally weak: just strong enough
to be rolled and shaped, but still brittle so that once baked it will break
apart easily into tender, melt-in-your-mouth flakes. To achieve this, the
gluten proteins in flour, which bind together to provide structure, must
be gently coaxed together and steps taken to minimize their strength.

1 Rubbing together the flour and fat is not
just a means of mixing ingredients. As you
rub, you are coating a proportion of the flour
particles with fat, and this will inhibit the
formation of glutens in the dough.

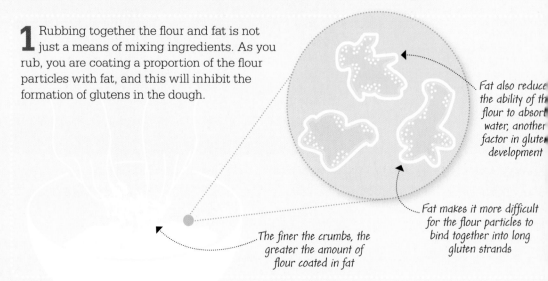

*Fat also reduces
the ability of the
flour to absorb
water, another
factor in gluten
development*

*Fat makes it more difficult
for the flour particles to
bind together into long
gluten strands*

*The finer the crumbs, the
greater the amount of
flour coated in fat*

2 Water must be mixed into flour before
gluten can start to form. Less water means
less gluten and this is why only a small amount
of water is added to pie dough, a little at
a time, and enough for the mixture to just
hold together in a ball.

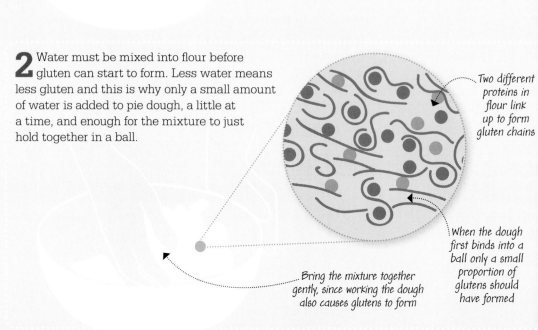

*Two different
proteins in
flour link
up to form
gluten chains*

*When the dough
first binds into a
ball only a small
proportion of
glutens should
have formed*

*Bring the mixture together
gently, since working the dough
also causes glutens to form*

3 Pie dough should only be lightly kneaded, if at all. Before it is flexible enough to roll out, more glutens are required to give the dough elasticity, but the baker must let time do most of the work.

More gluten strands form as flour in the drier pockets of dough absorbs water

The dough is left to "rest" for at least 30 minutes, wrapped in plastic wrap so it doesn't dry out

Water moves throughout the resting dough until it is evenly distributed

Gluten has time to relax so that when the dough is rolled out it doesn't spring back and won't shrink in the oven

Resting the dough in the fridge stops the fat from melting, which can make the dough greasy

4 The fat content in the dough plays another crucial role in achieving a light, flaky texture to the cooked pie crust. In the heat of the oven, the relatively large pieces of fat melt and leave behind pockets of air.

Different sized chunks of fat leave irregular spaces between layers of dough

Avoid stretching the dough as you line the pan, since this will cause the glutens to tighten more in the heat of the oven and cause shrinkage

Some of the air pockets left by the melted fat are expanded by vaporizing water in the dough

In the high heat of the oven the gluten and starch quickly set to hold the shape of the dough as the fat melts

Swiss Chard and Gruyère Tart

Perfect for a picnic or a lazy summer lunch, this tart is
equally delicious served hot or cold. To create a light and
crispy pastry, keep the dough cool, work quickly, and use
the lightest of touches. Don't forget that you can always
use spinach if you can't find Swiss chard.

✳

| Serves 6–8 | Bakes in 30–40 minutes | Up to 8 weeks |

Ingredients

For the pastry

osp unsalted butter, chilled and cubed

cup all-purpose flour, plus extra for dusting

gg yolk

For the filling

osp extra virgin olive oil

nion, finely chopped

a salt

arlic cloves, finely chopped

ew sprigs of fresh rosemary, eaves, picked and finely chopped

z (250g) Swiss chard or spinach, stems emoved and leaves coarsely chopped

z (125g) Gruyère cheese, grated

z (125g) feta cheese, cubed

shly ground black pepper

arge eggs, lightly beaten

cup whipping cream

Special Equipment

9in (23cm) tart pan with removable bottom

baking beans

all-purpose flour

olive oil

egg yolk

beaten eggs

unsalted butter

onion   **sea salt**   **garlic**   **rosemary**   **whipping cream**

Swiss chard or spinach

Gruyère cheese   **feta cheese**

black pepper

tart pan

baking beans

Total time *2 hours 20 minutes–2 hours 35 minutes, including 1 hour chilling time*

Prepare
5 minutes

Make *45–50 minutes*
+ 1 hour chilling

Bake
30–40 minutes

1 To make the dough, rub the butter and flour together until the mixture forms fine crumbs. Beat the egg yolk with 1 tbsp of cold water and add it to the crumb mixture.

Remember Make sure your hands are cold before rubbing in the butter. Run them under cold water for a minute, drying them afterward. Or, press your hands against an ice cooler block.

Use your fingertips to rub the flour and butter together to keep the mix as cool as possible

Quickly shape your dough into a very rough ball to keep from overworking it

2 Using a round-bladed knife to minimize contact with your hands, stir the egg mixture into the crumbs until you can bring the mixture together to form a soft dough. Quickly shape the dough into a ball, drawing in the crumbs from the sides of the bowl, too.

Careful! Add only enough egg mixture to form a soft but not sticky dough. It doesn't matter if you don't use all the egg.

3 Wrap the ball of dough in plastic wrap and chill in the fridge for 1 hour. Preheat the oven to 350°F (180°C). Gently roll out the dough, making sure you don't press down too hard, until approximately ⅛in (3mm) thick.

Why? Chilling the dough will help to relax it and prevent it from shrinking during baking.

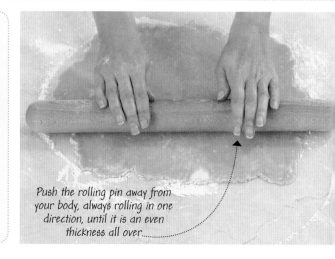

Push the rolling pin away from your body, always rolling in one direction, until it is an even thickness all over

4 Carefully fold the dough over the rolling pin, then gently lift the dough on to your tart pan and unwrap it over the pan. Line the pan by pushing the dough in with your fingers and leaving at least ¾in (2cm) of the dough hanging over the edges.

Why? Leave an overhang of dough in case the dough shrinks slightly on baking. You can trim off the excess dough once baked.

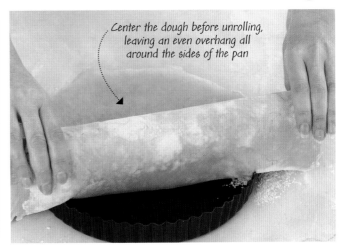

Center the dough before unrolling, leaving an even overhang all around the sides of the pan

Lightly prick all over the bottom, just so you leave an indentation with a fork but don't go all the way through

You can use ordinary dried beans or uncooked rice instead of baking beans

5 Lightly prick the bottom of the pie crust with a fork and place the pan on a baking sheet. Line the pan with parchment paper and fill it with baking beans.

Why? Pricking the dough with a fork prevents it from bubbling up as it cooks. Baking beans weigh the dough down, making an even crust and preventing it from rising on baking.

6 Bake the tart shell for 20–25 minutes, remove the paper and beans, and bake for another 5 minutes to crisp up the shell. Trim the edges with a knife to remove the excess dough.

Why? Cooking the dough first without the filling, called "baking blind," keeps the shell crisp. Cooking the shell with the filling would take too long, causing the filling to overcook or even burn.

Trim away from the pan to avoid getting crumbs in the shell

121

7 Pour the oil into a frying pan. Fry the onion with a pinch of salt over low heat for 2–3 minutes. Add the garlic and rosemary and cook for a few seconds. Stir constantly to prevent burning. Add the Swiss chard and cook for about 5 minutes until it just wilts.

Careful! Don't overcook the Swiss chard, since it will release too much of its water and make the tart's filling very wet.

Stir to prevent burning and stop cooking as soon as the chard starts to wilt

8 Spoon the chard filling into the pastry shell and spread it evenly over the bottom of the tart. Scatter grated Gruyère all over and then dot with the feta cheese on the top. Season well.

Tip If preferred, you can crumble the feta cheese over the filling rather than adding it as cubes.

9 Beat the remaining eggs and whipping cream together using a fork, and carefully pour over the tart, so it doesn't just settle in the middle of the filling. Let it seep into the shell, then bake for 30–40 minutes, or until golden and just set. Let cool slightly before releasing from the pan.

Careful! To prevent spillage, place the tart on the baking sheet before you pour in the egg mixture.

The perfect **Swiss Chard and Gruyère Tart**

Your finished tart should have a crisp pastry shell and a firm, creamy filling.

Top is lightly caramelized

The Swiss chard is evenly dispersed with the feta cheese

The egg cream mix has set, and the filling isn't wet

Thin, crisp, golden pastry

Did anything go wrong?

The pastry shell has shrunk. You may have added too much liquid to the dough or you didn't chill the pastry for long enough before baking. It needs to chill for at least 1 hour in the fridge.

The filling is very wet and not set. You may have overcooked the Swiss chard. If the chard gives off liquid, drain it off before you add it to the pastry shell.

The filling has started to seep out of the shell. When pricking the uncooked pastry shell, you may have pricked all the way through to the metal pan. Make sure you only lightly prick the pastry.

The filling is dry and very rubbery. You may have overcooked the tart. Since some ovens are naturally hotter than others, check the tart after 30 minutes to see if it is ready. You know the tart is ready when the middle of the filling has just set.

Try more Tarts ▶ ▶ ▶

Quiche Lorraine

Serves 4–6

Bakes in 25–30 minutes

Up to 8 weeks, baked

Ingredients

1⅓ cups all-purpose flour, plus extra for dusting

8 tbsp unsalted butter, cubed

1 large egg yolk

7oz (200g) thick-cut bacon, cut into ½in cubes

1 onion, finely chopped

3oz (75g) Gruyère cheese, grated

4 large eggs, lightly beaten

⅔ cup heavy cream

⅔ cup milk

freshly ground black pepper

Special Equipment

9 x 1½in (23 x 4cm) deep tart pan

baking beans or dried beans

MAKE THE PIE DOUGH

Sift the flour into a bowl, add the cubed butter, and, using your fingertips, rub the butter in until the mixture looks like bread crumbs. Then add the egg yolk and 3–4 tablespoons cold water or enough to make a smooth, but not sticky, dough. Wrap in plastic wrap and chill for 30 minutes. Preheat the oven to 375°F (190°C).

Roll the pie dough out on a lightly floured surface and use it to line the pan, trimming off any excess. Prick the bottom gently with a fork, then line with parchment paper and baking beans. Bake blind for 12 minutes. Remove the paper and beans, and bake for another 10 minutes, or until golden brown and cooked through.

Why? Baking your pie dough blind ensures that the pie crust will remain crisp once it has been baked with the filling in it.

MAKE THE FILLING AND BAKE

Heat a frying pan and dry fry the bacon for 3–5 minutes; it will release its fat. Add the onion and fry for another 2–3 minutes until softened slightly. Place the cooked pie crust on a baking sheet before adding the bacon and onion filling. Scatter the bacon and onion into the pie crust with the cheese.

Remember Scatter the bacon and onion evenly into the pie crust, otherwise you will end up with an unevenly filled quiche.

Beat together the eggs, cream, milk, and pepper to taste, then pour into the crust. Bake in the oven for 25–30 minutes, or until just set and golden brown. Remove from the oven and let cool very slightly before cutting into slices.

Onion Tart

Serves 6

Bakes in 15–20 minutes

Up to 8 weeks, baked

Ingredients

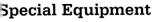

⅓ cups all-purpose flour, plus extra for dusting

tbsp unsalted butter, cubed

large egg yolk

tbsp olive oil

onions, sliced

tbsp all-purpose flour

¼ cups milk

tsp mild paprika

salt and freshly ground black pepper

Special Equipment

in (23cm) tart pan with removable bottom

baking beans or dried beans

MAKE THE PIE DOUGH AND FILLING

Sift the flour into a bowl, add the cubed butter, and, using your fingertips, rub the butter in until the mixture looks like bread crumbs. Add the egg yolk and 3–4 tablespoons cold water or enough to make a smooth, but not sticky, dough. Wrap in plastic wrap and chill for 30 minutes. Preheat the oven to 400°F (200°C).

Heat the oil in a nonstick frying pan. Add the onions and sweat very gently for 10–15 minutes, stirring constantly, until the onions are soft and translucent.

Careful! Cook the onions over low heat, since you want them softened but not colored.

Remove from the heat and stir in the flour. Add a little of the milk, and stir well. Return to the heat, add the rest of the milk, and heat gently, stirring constantly until the mixture thickens.

Why? Adding a small amount of milk to the flour allows you to make a smooth paste, which then makes it easier to mix in the remaining milk without any lumps forming.

Stir in 1 teaspoon of the paprika, season well, and set aside.

MAKE THE PIE DOUGH AND BAKE

On a lightly floured surface, roll the pie dough out and use it to line the pan, trimming off any excess. Prick the bottom gently with a fork, then line with parchment paper and baking beans. Bake the pie dough blind for 12 minutes. Remove paper and beans and bake for another 10 minutes, or until golden in color and cooked through. Remove from the oven and place on a baking sheet before filling with the onion mixture. Reduce the oven temperature to 350°F (180°C). Carefully spoon the filling into the pie crust, sprinkle over the remaining paprika, and bake in the oven for 15–20 minutes, or until just set and golden brown. Cool slightly before cutting into slices and serving.

Remember Since this tart is not made with eggs, the filling will not set firm and will have more of an open texture.

How to make **Sweet Pie Dough**

Sweet pie dough is crispier and more delicate than standard
pie dough because it is made with extra butter and more
egg yolk. The dough is sweetened with sugar and has a delicious,
crumbly texture after it is baked. This does not make the dough harder
to work with, provided it is properly chilled before you roll it out.

Egg yolks give richness and color to the mix

Sweetening and enriching the dough

Add sugar to your rubbed-in butter and flour
mix to sweeten the dough. Then add beaten
egg yolks and a little cold water, if needed.

The fat in the yolk, with the butter, acts as a
shortening agent, keeping the gluten in the
dough from linking and givng a crumbly texture

Wrapping the dough in plastic wrap will protect it from drying out in the fridge

Relaxing the dough

It is especially important to chill
sweet pie dough, since it is fragile
and tricky to roll out if not chilled
enough. Chilling allows the
dough's gluten to relax and
prevents it from shrinking during
baking. If the dough does begin
to fall apart on rolling out, don't
worry—carefully drape it over the
rolling pin, transfer to the pan and
press into the bottom, pinching
together any cracks and
smoothing over the surface so
there are no gaps in the dough.

ow to make **Crème Pâtissière**

ème pâtissière is a classic pastry cream—a little like a very thick
.stard—that is used in fresh fruit tarts and other desserts. It is
ickened with cornstarch and, unlike custard, it won't separate when
oked, but it requires careful attention and constant whisking to ensure
remains smooth and thickened enough without any lumps forming.

... Whisk all the time as you pour in the milk

Making the crème base

Since your crème pâtissière must be thick and
very creamy, you must whisk your ingredients
or the crème base until very smooth. You first
make a batterlike base from flour, eggs, and
sugar. Whisk until very smooth before pouring
in the heated milk, whisking constantly.

Custard is very thick when ready ....

Tip To cool, spoon
the crème into a
bowl and top with a
round of wax paper
to prevent a skin
from forming.

Cooking the crème

Gently cook the crème over low
heat, for about 3 minutes, whisking
constantly with a handheld whisk,
until it changes from a thin to a
very thick, smooth consistency. To
test if the crème is ready, remove
the whisk—if it leaves a thick trail
that won't disappear, the creme is
ready. Continuous whisking will
also prevent the crème from
curdling and sticking to the pan.
Make sure you cook the crème in
advance because it needs to be
thoroughly chilled before use.

Strawberry Tart

| Serves 6–8 | Bakes in 25 minutes | Up to 12 weeks, unfilled |

Ingredients

7 tbsp unsalted butter, chilled and cubed

1¼ cups all-purpose flour, plus extra for dusting

¾ cup sugar

1 large egg yolk, plus 2 whole large eggs

1½ tsp pure vanilla extract

6 tbsp red currant jelly, for glazing

½ cup cornstarch

1¾ cups whole milk

10oz (300g) strawberries, hulled and thickly sliced

Special Equipment

9in (23cm) tart pan with removable bottom

baking beans or dried beans

MAKE AND BAKE THE PIE DOUGH

Rub the butter into the sifted flour until the mixture resembles bread crumbs. Stir in ¼ cup sugar. Beat together the egg yolk and ½ tsp vanilla, and mix into the flour mixture with a little water, if needed, to form a soft dough. Wrap in plastic wrap and chill for 1 hour. Preheat the oven to 350°F (180°C). On a lightly floured surface, roll the pie dough out to ⅛in (3mm) thickness. Line the pan with the pie dough, trimming off any excess. Prick the bottom gently with a fork, line with parchment paper and baking beans, and place on a baking sheet. Blind bake for 20 minutes, remove the paper and beans, and bake again for 5 minutes. Melt the jelly with 1 tbsp water, then brush a little over the pie crust and cool.

Why? Brushing with melted red currant jelly creates a sweet glaze that will help to stop the pie crust from getting soggy when the filling is added.

MAKE THE FILLING

To make the crème pâtissière, beat the remaining sugar, cornstarch, eggs, and 1 tsp vanilla together in a bowl. Heat the milk in a saucepan to just below a boil. Pour into the egg mixture, whisking constantly. Return the crème to the pan and cook over medium heat, whisking constantly for 4–5 minutes, or until thickened. Reduce the heat and cook for 2–3 minutes over low heat. Transfer to a bowl, cover with plastic wrap, and cool completely.

ASSEMBLE AND SERVE

Beat the cooled crème pâtissière until smooth, then spread it over the pie crust to produce an even layer. Top with the strawberries, arranging them in circles starting from the outside edge and working into the center. Heat the jelly mixture again until runny then brush over the strawberries and let set. Carefully remove the tart from the pan and place on a serving plate

Remember To save time, the crème pâtissière can be made a day ahead and cooled overnight. Just make sure you beat it well to soften it slightly before spreading it into the pie crust.

Raspberry Tart with Chocolate Cream

Serves 6–8

Bakes in 20–25 minutes

Up to 12 weeks, unfilled

Ingredients

1 cup all-purpose flour, plus extra for dusting

¼ cup cocoa powder

7 tbsp unsalted butter, chilled and cubed

¼ cup sugar

1 large egg yolk, plus 2 large whole eggs

1½ tsp pure vanilla extract

½ cup cornstarch

1¾ cups whole milk

6oz (175g) good-quality dark chocolate, broken into pieces

14oz (400g) raspberries

confectioners' sugar, for dusting

Special Equipment

9in (23cm) tart pan with removable bottom

baking beans or dried beans

MAKE AND BAKE THE PIE DOUGH

Sift the flour and cocoa into a bowl. Add the butter and rub in until the mixture looks like bread crumbs. Stir in ¼ cup of the sugar. Beat together the egg yolk and ½ tsp vanilla, add to the flour mixture, and form a soft dough; add water, if a little dry. Wrap in plastic wrap and chill for 1 hour. Preheat the oven to 350°F (180°C). On a lightly floured surface, roll the pie dough out to ⅛in (3mm) thickness and line the pan with it, trimming off any excess. Prick the bottom gently with a fork, line with parchment paper and baking beans, and place on a baking sheet. Bake for 20 minutes, remove the paper and beans, and bake for another 5 minutes, until cooked through. Remove from the oven and let cool.

MAKE THE FILLING

Beat the remaining sugar, cornstarch, eggs, and 1 tsp vanilla in a bowl. Bring the milk and 4oz (100g) chocolate to just below a boil, whisking all the time until the chocolate has melted. Pour the hot milk onto the egg mixture, whisking nonstop. Then return the chocolate crème to the pan and cook over medium heat for 4–5 minutes, or until thickened, whisking all the time. Reduce the heat to low and cook for another 2–3 minutes, whisking constantly. Transfer the chocolate crème to a bowl, cover with plastic wrap to prevent a skin from forming, and cool completely.

ASSEMBLE AND SERVE

Melt the remaining chocolate in a heatproof bowl set over a pan of simmering water. Brush over the cooked pie crust and let set. Remove the pie crust from the pan and arrange it on a serving plate. Beat the chilled chocolate crème until smooth, then spoon into the crust. Top with the raspberries and lightly dust with confectioners' sugar using a fine sieve.

Tip You can prepare the pie dough and crème pâtissière a day ahead, but the prepared tart is best eaten the same day.

How to make **Double-crust Sweet Pies**

Double-crust sweet pies are deep-filled fruit pies that are lined with a sweet pie crust and topped with a lid, giving you the "double crust." Unlike tarts, you don't blind bake the crust of a double-crust pie, since it is first cooked at a higher temperature to firm up the pie crust and lid. You then reduce the heat and bake it for longer to finish the cooking process. A double-crust pie crust, however, will never be as crispy or dry as a tart's crust.

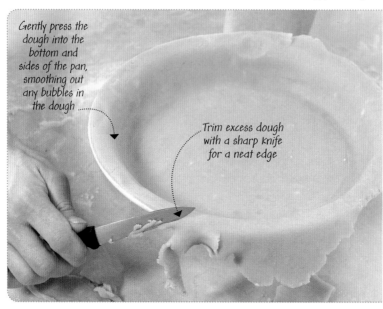

Gently press the dough into the bottom and sides of the pan, smoothing out any bubbles in the dough

Trim excess dough with a sharp knife for a neat edge

Lining the pie pan

On a lightly floured surface, roll out half of the dough to a circle about 2in (5cm) wider than the pie pan, so you have enough dough to line the pan. Drape the dough over the pan, then press it into the bottom and sides, trimming any excess at the edge of the pan at a slight angle. This helps reduce shrinkage as it bakes.

Egg wash creates a seal

Use a rolling pin to transfer and unwrap the dough

Filling and topping the pie

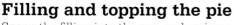

Spoon the filling into the pan and, using a pastry brush, brush the rim of the crust with beaten egg, known as egg wash. Roll out the remaining dough and use it to top the pie. Press the edges together to seal, then flute the edge with the back of a knife (see p.69).

Apple Pie

**Serves
6–8**

**Bakes in
50–55
minutes**

**Unsuitable
for freezing**

Ingredients

2½ cups all-purpose flour, plus extra

½ tsp salt

¼ cup vegetable shortening, plus extra
for greasing

½ cup sugar, plus extra

2¼lb (1kg) tart apples, peeled, cored, and cut
into medium slices

Juice of 1 lemon

½ tsp ground cinnamon, or to taste

¼ tsp grated nutmeg, or to taste

1 large egg, beaten, to brush

1 tbsp milk, for glazing

Grease a 9in (23cm) round, shallow pie pan.

MAKE THE PIE DOUGH

Sift the flour and salt into a bowl, add the
shortening, and rub in until the mixture resembles
bread crumbs. Stir in 2 tablespoons sugar, then add
6 tablespoons cold water, or just enough, to bring the
mixture together to form a soft dough. Shape into a
ball, wrap in plastic wrap, and chill for 30 minutes.

ASSEMBLE THE PIE

Roll out half of the dough on a lightly floured
surface. Use the dough to line the pan, gently
pressing into the bottom and up the sides. Trim off
any excess dough and chill for 15 minutes. Place
apple slices in a bowl with the lemon juice and
toss until well coated. Sprinkle in 2 tablespoons
flour, ½ cup sugar, cinnamon, and nutmeg, and
stir until well mixed.

Why? Adding flour to the apple mix slightly
thickens up the juices in the filling during baking.

Spoon the apple mix into the pie pan, filling
more in the center so that you create a slight mound.
Brush the dough on the edge of the pan with the
egg wash and roll out the remaining dough to cover
the pie completely. Lift the dough onto the pie pan
and trim off any excess. Press the edges together to
seal, crimping the edges as you go. Cut an "X" in
the middle of the crust and pull back the point of
each triangle to reveal the filling. If you like, decorate
the pie with strips of dough trimmings, using a
little water to secure. Brush the top with the milk,
sprinkle over a little sugar, and chill for 30 minutes.
Preheat the oven to 425°F (220°C).

BAKE AND SERVE

Bake the pie for 20 minutes, then reduce
the temperature to 350°F (180°C), and bake for
another 30–35 minutes, or until crisp and golden
brown. Cover loosely with foil if the pie starts
browning too much. Serve warm.

Rhubarb and Strawberry variations Mix
together the following for the filling: 2¼lb (1kg)
sliced rhubarb, finely grated zest of 1 orange, 1 cup
sugar, and ¼ tsp salt. Stir in 13oz (375g) hulled and
halved strawberries. Spoon into the dough-lined
pie pan. Dot 1 tbsp cubed butter over the filling,
then continue as in the recipe.

How to make **Yeast-risen Bread**

Yeast-risen breads need flour with a higher gluten content to produce a good bread structure and rely on yeast to make them rise. To create a well-risen loaf, you must rehydrate the yeast ("proof it"), knead the dough to stretch and develop the gluten within it, leave it to rise, then "punch down" the air from the dough, and proof it for one final rise before baking.

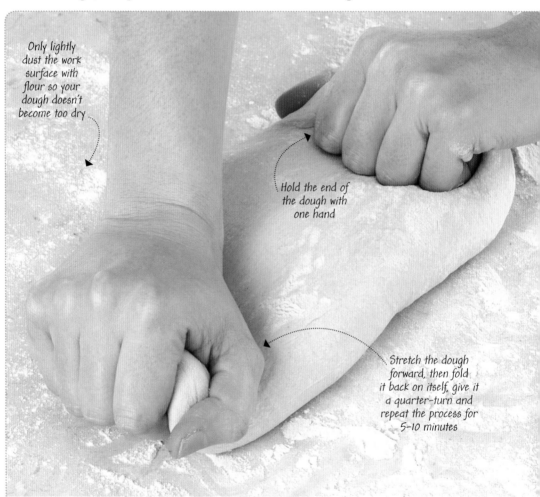

Only lightly dust the work surface with flour so your dough doesn't become too dry

Hold the end of the dough with one hand

Stretch the dough forward, then fold it back on itself, give it a quarter-turn and repeat the process for 5–10 minutes

Kneading the dough

Kneading stretches the dough and develops the gluten in the flour, helping the loaf rise. Keep turning the dough by a quarter-turn each time you push it forward and fold it back on itself. This will ensure the gluten is evenly formed and the yeast well-distributed. If you don't knead your dough well enough, you'll end up with a poorly risen loaf. Your dough is ready when it is smooth and "springs back" when pressed with a finger.

Leaving the dough to rise

Leave your dough to rise in a warm place for an hour or so until it doubles in size. Leaving your dough in a cool environment will slow down the rising process considerably. Rising allows the ingredients to work together to produce carbon dioxide, while the developing gluten enables the dough to stretch, which traps carbon dioxide in the mix. On baking, the gas evaporates from the dough to leave a well-risen bread with a light texture.

Plastic wrap creates a warm, moist environment that allows the dough to rise and prevents it from drying out

It's best to cover the bowl with plastic wrap but a clean dish towel will do

Always put the dough in a lightly oiled bowl to prevent it from sticking

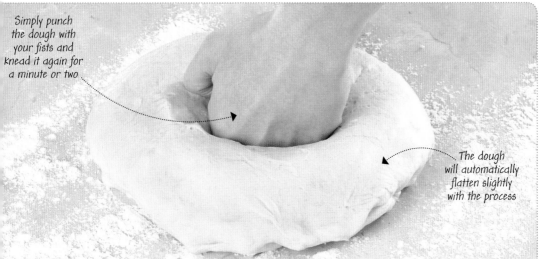

Simply punch the dough with your fists and knead it again for a minute or two

The dough will automatically flatten slightly with the process

Punching down the dough

You need to punch down the newly risen dough to remove any excess carbon dioxide and knead it again briefly to redistribute the yeast within the dough. You then need to shape the dough and leave it to proof for one final rise before baking.

The science of Baking Bread

The chemical process going on inside fermenting bread dough is in essence the same as for brewing beer. In both instances, yeast is encouraged to feed on the sugars in processed grain to produce carbon dioxide gas and alcohol. Key to bread-making is to trap this gas inside the dough and use it to create the wonderfully light texture of bread.

1 Only three ingredients are needed for bread: flour, yeast, and water. Yeast is a microscopic living organism, a kind of fungi, with an ability to ferment the sugars in flour.

Water hotter than 113°F (45°C) will inhibit yeast activity; above 140°F (60°C) and the yeast will die

Water is absorbed by the starch content in flour and enzymes then begin to break down the starch into sugars for the yeast to feed on

Recipes call for lukewarm water, since this helps create the optimum temperature in the dough for yeast to thrive: 77–86°F (25–30°C)

2 Unlike cake mix and pie dough, bread dough must be worked on vigorously—"kneaded"— to encourage the formation of glutens that will give the dough its vital elasticity.

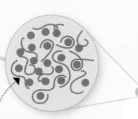

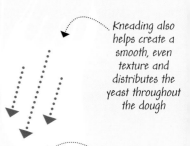

Kneading also helps create a smooth, even texture and distributes the yeast throughout the dough

Kneading encourages more proteins to combine into gluten, which link up into a stretchy, elastic structure

Gluten is made from two different proteins in flour that start to combine with each other as soon as water is added

The dough is ready when you can stretch it without tearing

3 The yeast is then left to do its business of converting sugar into carbon dioxide gas and alcohol. The gas stretches the elastic dough but cannot escape and so forms lots of small pockets in the dough.

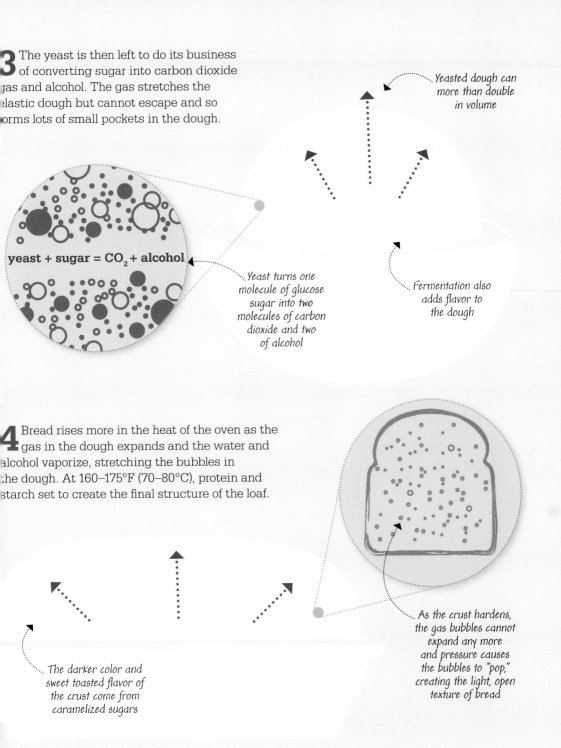

Yeasted dough can more than double in volume

yeast + sugar = CO_2 + alcohol

Yeast turns one molecule of glucose sugar into two molecules of carbon dioxide and two of alcohol

Fermentation also adds flavor to the dough

4 Bread rises more in the heat of the oven as the gas in the dough expands and the water and alcohol vaporize, stretching the bubbles in the dough. At 160–175°F (70–80°C), protein and starch set to create the final structure of the loaf.

As the crust hardens, the gas bubbles cannot expand any more and pressure causes the bubbles to "pop," creating the light, open texture of bread

The darker color and sweet toasted flavor of the crust come from caramelized sugars

Rosemary Focaccia

Focaccia is an Italian bread made with yeast-risen dough enriched and flavored with olive oil, and topped with herbs. Focaccia dough is well-tempered and easy to make, so it's a perfect recipe for a novice.

Serves 6–8	Bakes in 15–20 minutes	Unsuitable for freezing

ingredients

bsp dried yeast

cups flour,
plus extra for dusting

sp salt

ves from 5–7 sprigs of rosemary,
two-thirds finely chopped

cup extra virgin olive oil, plus extra
for greasing

tsp freshly ground black pepper

a salt flakes

pecial Equipment

x 9in (38 x 23cm) jelly roll pan

all-purpose flour

dried yeast

salt and sea salt flakes

olive oil   **rosemary**   **black pepper**

jelly roll pan

Total time *2 hours 20 minutes–3 hours 10 minutes, including 1½–2¼ hours rising time*

Prepare
5 minutes

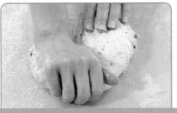

Make
30 minutes + rising time

Bake
15–20 minutes

1 Proof the yeast by sprinkling it over 4 tablespoons lukewarm water and letting it stand for 5 minutes. Sift the flour and salt into a large bowl, making a well in the center. Add the chopped rosemary, yeast mix, 4 tablespoons olive oil, and 1 cup lukewarm water. Gradually draw in the flour and work into a smooth dough.

Careful! Use lukewarm water to soak the yeast; hot water will kill it.

After proofing, the yeast mixture will look frothy and bubbly

The dough will have a smooth, elastic texture when ready and will spring back when pressed with a finger

2 Turn the dough onto a floured surface and knead for 5–7 minutes. Shape it into a round, which aids rising, then place in a lightly oiled bowl, cover, and leave to rise for 1–1½ hours until doubled in size. Turn it onto a work surface again and punch down the air by punching the dough with your fists. Knead very briefly, then cover again, and let rest for another 5 minutes.

3 Lightly grease your jelly roll pan. Place your dough in the pan and flatten it out, filling the pan evenly. Cover with a dish towel and leave it to rise again for 35–45 minutes until the dough puffs up a little.

Why? The dough needs to rise a final time so that it puffs up enough for you to make dimples in it.

Press the dough right into the edges—you may need to be firm as an elastic dough might spring back

4 Preheat the oven to 400°F (200°C). Scatter the remaining rosemary leaves and the pepper over the top of the dough. Poke the dough all over to make deep dimples, drizzle the remaining oil over, and scatter with the sea salt flakes. Bake for 15–20 minutes until browned.

Why? Dimples prevent the dough from rising up too much during baking.

To make dimples, poke the dough evenly all over with your fingertips

The perfect **Rosemary Focaccia**

The perfect focaccia will be lightly browned, evenly risen with a thickness of about ¾in (2cm), and will have a light and airy texture.

Did anything go wrong?

The focaccia hasn't risen very well. You may not have given the dough enough time to rise. The dough needs to be left to rise to allow the yeast to work properly.

The focaccia has risen unevenly. To avoid this, the dough needs to be evenly spread out in the baking pan.

The focaccia is very tough and heavy. You may not have kneaded the dough enough to allow the gluten to develop. Next time, knead your dough for as much as 10 minutes and ensure you really are stretching the dough.

The rosemary on top of the focaccia is burned. The temperature of your oven may have been too high.

The olive oil will have soaked into the holes in the top of the focaccia and into the bread

Crisp crust

Evenly spaced dimples

Light crumb

Try more Yeast-risen Bread recipes ▶ ▶ ▶

White Loaf

1 loaf

Bakes in 40–45 minutes

Up to 4 weeks

Ingredients

4 cups bread flour, plus extra for dusting

1 tsp fine salt

2 tsp dried yeast

1 tbsp sunflower or vegetable oil, plus extra for greasing

MAKE THE DOUGH

Sift the flour and salt into a bowl. In a separate small bowl dissolve the yeast in 1¼ cups warm water and, once dissolved, add the oil to it.

Careful! Dissolve the yeast in lukewarm water—any hotter and it will kill the yeast.

Make a well in the center of the flour, pour in the yeast mixture, and stir to form a rough dough. Bring the dough together, turn out onto a lightly floured surface and knead well for 10 minutes until smooth. Place the dough in a lightly oiled bowl, cover loosely with a clean dish cloth, and leave to rise in a warm place for up to 2 hours, or until doubled in size. Turn the dough onto the work surface and punch it down to its original size. Knead it until smooth.

SHAPE AND BAKE THE BREAD

Shape the dough into a long, curved, oblong shape. Place on a baking sheet, cover with plastic wrap and a dish towel, and leave in a warm place for about an hour, or until doubled in size. Preheat the oven to 425°F (220°C) and arrange the oven shelves so that there is one at the very bottom of the oven and one in the middle.

Slash the top of the risen loaf diagonally 2 or 3 times with a sharp knife—this allows the dough to continue to rise in the oven. Dust the top of the loaf with flour. Place the loaf on the middle shelf. Quickly place a roasting pan on the bottom shelf and pour some boiling water into it, and shut the oven door.

Why? Placing the sheet of boiling water in the oven creates plenty of steam while baking, which helps the bread to rise and get a crisp crust.

Bake the bread for 10 minutes, then reduce the heat to 375°F (190°C) and bake for another 30–35 minutes until the crust is browned and the loaf sounds hollow when tapped. Remove from the oven and let cool on a wire rack.

Walnut and Rosemary variation After the dough has been punched down, gently knead in 1½ cups chopped walnuts and 3 tablespoons finely chopped rosemary. Halve the dough and shape each half into a 6in (15cm) round. Arrange on a baking sheet, cover with a dish towel, and let rise for 30 minutes. When the dough has doubled in size, brush with oil and then bake as in the recipe for 30–40 minutes.

Whole-wheat Cottage Loaf

2 loaves   **Bakes in 40–45 minutes**   **Up to 8 weeks**

Ingredients

3 tbsp honey

3 tsp dried yeast

4 tbsp unsalted butter, melted, plus
   extra for greasing

1 tbsp salt

5 cups stone-ground whole-wheat flour

¾ cup all-purpose flour, plus
   extra for dusting

MAKE THE DOUGH

Mix 1 tablespoon honey and 4 tablespoons of lukewarm water in a bowl, then sprinkle the yeast over the top and leave to dissolve for 5 minutes, stirring once. In a large bowl mix the melted butter, yeast mixture, salt, remaining honey, and 1½ cup lukewarm water. Stir in half the whole-wheat flour with all the white flour and mix well. Add the remaining whole-wheat flour ¾ cup at a time, mixing well after each addition. The dough should be soft and slightly sticky.

Turn the dough out onto a lightly floured surface and knead for 10 minutes until it is very smooth and elastic. Place the dough in a lightly buttered bowl and toss the dough around to butter its surface slightly. Cover with a damp dish towel and leave in a warm place for 1–1½ hours or until doubled in size.

Why? Yeast works more efficiently in a warm environment, so speeding up the rising process.

SHAPE AND BAKE THE DOUGH

Turn the dough out onto the work surface and punch down the air. Cover and let rest for 5 minutes, then cut into 3 equal pieces; cut one

of the pieces in half. Shape one of the larger pieces into a tight ball by smoothing it into a round, pulling any seams underneath the dough, and place seam-side-down on a lightly greased baking sheet. Then shape one of the smaller pieces into a smaller ball, as before, and sit it seam-side-down on top of the first ball. Using your finger, press through the center of the balls right down to the baking sheet. Repeat this process with the remaining dough for the second loaf.

Cover the loaves with dish towels and leave in a warm place for 45 minutes or until doubled in size. Preheat the oven to 375°F (190°C). Bake the loaves for 40–45 minutes or until well browned. Let cool on a wire rack.

Remember When cooked through, the loaves should sound hollow when the bottom is tapped.

How to make **Pizza Dough**

Making deliciously light and well-risen pizza dough doesn't have to be a time-consuming task. Prepare the dough a day in advance and place it in the fridge to rise overnight. The next day, all you have to do is roll it out—although the tricky part is achieving a good circle without knocking all the air out—before you top it and bake to perfection.

Tip The gluten in pizza dough gives it elasticity but sometimes makes it tricky to shape. If this happens, let the dough rest for 5 minutes, so the gluten relaxes, and try again.

Roll gently to keep from rolling out all the air pockets from the dough

Rolling out the pizza dough

On a lightly floured surface, gently stretch your dough into a rough circle. Using a rolling pin dusted lightly with flour, gently roll the dough from the center of the circle in one direction only, turning it 90° after each roll, until it forms a circle of your desired size.

Four Seasons Pizza

x 9in (23cm) pizzas | Bakes in 40 minutes | Unsuitable for freezing

Ingredients

3 tsp dried yeast

5 tbsp olive oil, plus extra for greasing

2¾ cups bread flour,
   plus extra for dusting

½ tsp salt

2 tbsp unsalted butter

2 shallots, finely chopped

1 bay leaf

3 garlic cloves, crushed

2¼lb (1kg) ripe plum tomatoes,
   seeded and chopped

2 tbsp tomato paste

1 tbsp sugar

6oz (175g) mozzarella, thinly sliced

4oz (115g) mushrooms, thinly sliced

2 roasted red bell peppers, thinly sliced

8 anchovy fillets, halved lengthwise

4oz (115g) pepperoni, thinly sliced

2 tbsp capers

8 artichoke hearts, halved

12 pitted black olives

MAKE THE DOUGH

Dissolve the yeast in 1½ cups lukewarm water in a bowl, then stir in 2 tablespoons of the oil. Sift the flour and salt in a separate bowl, add the yeast mixture, and combine to form a dough. Knead the dough well on a lightly floured surface for 10 minutes, or until very smooth and elastic. Shape into a ball and place in a lightly oiled bowl covered with oiled plastic wrap. Leave in a warm place for 1–1½ hours until doubled in size.

MAKE THE SAUCE

Melt the butter in a saucepan, add the shallots, 1 tablespoon oil, bay leaf, and garlic, and fry gently for 5–6 minutes, stirring occasionally so the shallots and garlic don't color. Stir in the tomatoes, tomato paste, and sugar into the pan and cook for 5 minutes. Add 1 cup water, bring to a boil, reduce to simmer, and cook for 30 minutes, stirring occasionally until reduced to a thick sauce. Press the sauce through a sieve, season, and chill.

Why? Sieving helps produce a smoother sauce, and it needs to be thick so that the pizza isn't wet and the tomato sauce doesn't dominate the flavors.

ASSEMBLE AND BAKE

Preheat the oven to 400°F (200°C). Transfer the dough to a floured surface and knead lightly. Divide into 4 balls and roll into approximately 9in (23cm) rounds. Place each round on a greased baking sheet. Spread the sauce over the bases, leaving a ¾in (2cm) border around each. Divide the mozzarella evenly between the 4 bases. Place the mushrooms on a quarter of each pizza and brush with some olive oil. Place the pepper slices on another quarter and top with the anchovies. Top the remaining quarters equally with the pepperoni and capers and then the artichokes and olives. Bake 2 pizzas at a time in the oven for 20 minutes, or until golden brown. Serve hot.

How to make **Sweetened Breads**

Sweetened breads such as fruit buns are made from yeast-risen bread dough enriched with butter, milk, and sugar. These additions give the breads a better flavor and softer texture. The rising of the dough, which may be a little softer because of these additions, is the secret to their success, giving them a beautifully light feel.

Making a well in the center to add the yeast mixture makes mixing easier

Adding milk and yeast

For the dough to rise, you need to rehydrate or proof dried yeast by adding warm milk to it. Warm the milk gently until it is just warm enough for you to be able to put a finger in it—any hotter and it can kill the yeast. Then pour onto the yeast. Let the mix stand for 10 minutes until it becomes frothy. This is a good sign that your yeast is alive and active, before you add it to the other ingredients.

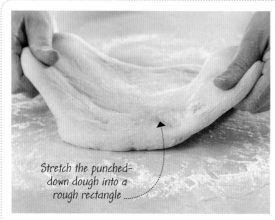

Stretch the punched-down dough into a rough rectangle

Scatter the fruit on top, fold the dough over, and knead

Adding fruit

Add the fruit after the dough has risen once and been punched down. At this stage, you shape the dough into a rough rectangle, scatter fruit on top, fold over, and gently knead in until the fruit is evenly mixed throughout. Then shape the dough, place it on a baking sheet, and leave to rise again for a final proof, or rise, before baking.

Spiced Fruit Buns

Makes 12 | **Bakes in 15 minutes** | **Up to 4 weeks**

Ingredients

1 cup tepid milk

2 tsp dried yeast

3¾ cups bread flour, sifted, plus extra for dusting

1 tsp pumpkin pie spice

½ tsp nutmeg

1 tsp salt

½ cup sugar

4 tbsp unsalted butter, cubed,
    plus extra for greasing

vegetable oil for greasing

1½ cups (6oz) mixed dried fruit (raisins, golden
    raisins, and mixed peel)

2 tbsp confectioners' sugar

¼ tsp pure vanilla extract

MAKE THE DOUGH

Warm the milk gently until lukewarm, stir in the yeast, cover, and leave for 10 minutes until frothy.

Careful! Heat the the milk to a tepid or lukewarm temperature, any hotter and it will kill off the yeast.

Sift together the flour, spices, salt, and sugar, and rub the butter in (see p.26) until the mixture resembles fine bread crumbs. Stir the yeast mixture into the flour mixture and bring together to form a soft dough. Turn the dough onto a lightly floured surface and knead well for 10 minutes. Shape into a ball, place in an oiled bowl, cover, and leave in a warm place to rise for 1 hour.

SHAPE THE DOUGH

Turn the risen dough on to a lightly floured surface, punch down, then shape into a rough rectangle. Scatter over the fruit, fold the dough over, and gently knead in the fruit until evenly mixed throughout.

Why? Knead the fruit into the dough only after the dough has risen once, otherwise it will become too heavy to rise properly.

Divide the dough into 12 pieces, roll into balls, and place them spaced well apart on greased baking sheets. Cover and leave in a warm place for 30 minutes or until doubled in size.

BAKE AND GLAZE

Preheat the oven to 400°F (200°C). Bake the buns for 15 minutes or until the buns sound hollow when tapped. Transfer to a wire rack to cool slightly. Before the buns cool completely, mix the confectioners' sugar, vanilla, and 1 tablespoon of cold water together in a bowl, then brush over the still warm buns to glaze them.

Tip These buns will keep very well for up to 2 days if stored in an airtight container.

3

Take It Further

Take your baking to the next level with a
final selection of recipes and techniques
that will test and build on your new skills.
Make sumptuous gâteau-style whisked
cakes, learn how to roll and fold dough
for light and buttery Danish pastries,
and impress your friends and family
with tangy artisan-style breads.

In this section, learn to bake:

Gâteau-style **Choux**
Cakes **Pastry**
pp.148–57 *pp.158–67*

Danish **Artisan**
Pastry **Breads**
pp.168–77 *pp.178–87*

How to make **Gâteau-style Cakes**

Gâteau-style cakes, which are usually layered with cream and fruit fillings, are the lightest cakes of all. Very little fat and no rising agent is added to these cakes, so it is vital to get a lot of air into the mix. This requires lengthy beating, preferably over gentle heat, and careful folding in of the flour so air is not lost.

Beat the mixture for at least 5 minutes, or until the volume has tripled in size

Use a bowl larger than the width of the pan so the bottom doesn't touch the water, which would "cook" the mixture

Tip You can check if your mixture has enough air in it by doing the "trail" test: lift out the beaters and if the drips from the beaters leave a distinct trail on the surface of the mix that doesn't disappear, then the mix is ready.

Beating eggs and sugar

Over a pan of simmering water, beat the eggs and sugar until very thick. Applying heat as you beat helps to dissolve the sugar and slightly thicken the eggs, which encourages the eggs and sugar mixture to hold on to the air bubbles created.

Remember to scrape down the sides of the bowl

Do not overmix the cake mixture, otherwise the cake will be flat and heavy

Adding the dry ingredients

With a large metal spoon or spatula, use figure-eight motion to fold in the flour. Firmly but gently draw spoonfuls of the dry ingredients down into the wet mix and then turn the wet mix back over the dry. Repeat until no trace of the dry ingredients remains.

Use your hands to support the fragile cake layer as you cut it

Cut with a gentle sawing motion using a long-bladed serrated knife held horizontally

Cutting the cake into layers

Mark out the layers on the cake before cutting. Don't rush and if it begins to slope bring the knife back on course. The best way to move the layers without them breaking is to place both hands under each layer to support the cake slice and carefully lift it into place.

Black Forest Gâteau

If any bake is sure to astonish and delight guests,
it's a creamy, layered gâteau. It might look tricky,
but just practice a few simple techniques and you
will achieve amazing results.

| Serves 8 | Bakes in 40 minutes | Up to 4 weeks |

Ingredients

bsp butter, melted, plus extra
or greasing

arge eggs, at room temperature

cup sugar

cup all-purpose flour

cup cocoa powder

sp pure vanilla extract

r the filling and decoration

14oz (425g) cans pitted black cherries,
drained thoroughly and patted dry
n paper towels, 6 tbsp juice reserved,
nd cherries from 1 can coarsely chopped

bsp Kirsch

ups heavy cream

z (150g) dark chocolate, finely grated

pecial Equipment

n (23cm) round springform cake pan

ping bag and large star nozzle

butter   **eggs**   **sugar**   **all-purpose flour**

cocoa powder   **vanilla extract**   **black cherries**   **kirsch**

heavy cream   **dark chocolate**   **piping bag with star nozzle**

Total time *1 hour 30 minutes, plus cooling*

| **Prepare** | **Make** | **Bake** | **Decorate** |
| *10 minutes* | *20 minutes* | *40 minutes* | *20 minutes* |

1 Preheat the oven to 350°F (180°C). Cut a strip of parchment paper 1¾in (4.5cm) deeper than the pan's height for the sides of the pan. Fold 1in (2.5cm) along one long edge of the paper, cut snips in it at a 45° angle, and line the side of the pan with the snipped edge at the bottom; the parchment will extend above the rim. Place the pan on parchment, draw a circle around the outside, cut the circle and line the bottom with it. Set aside.

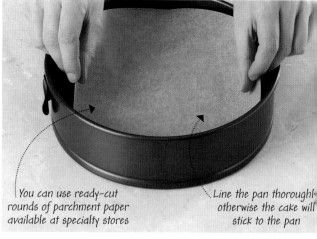

You can use ready-cut rounds of parchment paper available at specialty stores

Line the pan thoroughly otherwise the cake will stick to the pan

Beat the mixture until it holds a trail that doesn't disappear when the beaters are lifted

2 Beat the eggs and sugar in a bowl set over a pan of simmering water, until very thick and pale. Take off the heat and let cool slightly.

Careful! Keep the heat low and don't let the bottom of the bowl touch the water.

3 Sift the flour and cocoa together. Fold the dry ingredients into the beaten mixture very carefully so you don't knock any air out. Fold in the butter and vanilla extract.

Remember Fold very gently using a figure-eight motion to keep as much of the air you have just beaten into it. This will produce a light-textured cake.

The batter is ready when no flecks of flour or cocoa are visible

4 Spoon the mixture into the cake pan, smooth over the surface, and bake in the center of the oven for 40 minutes, or until well risen and just shrinking away from the sides. To test if the cake is done, insert a metal skewer into the center of the cake. If it comes out clean, the cake is done; if not, simply cook for a few minutes more and retest. Let cool slightly in the pan.

Level the surface with a spatula to prevent any peaking as it bakes

5 Transfer the cake to a wire rack and carefully remove the parchment paper. Let cool completely.

Why? Removing the parchment paper helps your cake to cool properly, and a wire rack allows air to circulate and steam to escape rather than condense as water, making the cake soggy.

6 Using a serrated knife, carefully cut the cake into 3 layers. Combine the reserved cherry juice and kirsch, and drizzle a third of the liquid over each cake layer.

Careful! Make sure you drizzle the juice and kirsch mixture evenly, otherwise parts of the cake will become soggy, causing it to collapse.

Divide the cake evenly and keep the knife completely level

7 Whip the cream until it just holds its shape. Arrange one cake layer on a serving plate and spread with a third of the whipped cream and half the chopped cherries. Repeat with the second layer, and top with the final layer.

Tip Divide the cream and cherries equally between the layers, but don't put on so much that the filling oozes out. A palette knife is the best tool to use here.

Carefully ease the layers or top, not pressing down as yo could push out the filling

Coat only the sides with cream, making sure you don't get any on the top

Scatter grated chocolate onto a palette knife, then carefully press into the sides until all the cream is covered in chocolate

8 Spread the sides of the cake with some of the whipped cream. Using a palette knife, gently press the grated chocolate into the cream around the sides of the cake.

Careful! Spread the cream gently onto the cake sides, since you don't want any cake crumbs in the cream.

9 Place the piping bag in a glass to support it, fold down the sides slightly, and spoon the remaining cream into the bag. Pipe rosettes around the edge of the cake by holding the piping bag over the cake, one hand at the top and one at the bottom, and gently squeeze the top of the bag until you've delivered a perfect cream swirl. Place cherries in the center and sprinkle grated chocolate over the cream rosettes.

The cherries should be well drained, otherwis they will make th cake soggy

The perfect **Black Forest Gâteau**

The finished gâteau will be deliciously light and airy with mouthwatering layers of cream and cherries.

Finely grated chocolate tops the swirls of cream

Succulent layers of whipped cream laced with chopped cherries

Deliciously light and airy layers of cake

Did anything go wrong?

The egg and sugar mixture looks like it has separated. Your bowl has touched the water in the pan underneath and caused the eggs to curdle.

The cake is very flat. You didn't beat the egg and sugar mixture for long enough.

There are white specks in the cooked cake. You didn't mix in the flour properly.

The sides of the cake are wet. The cake has been left to cool for too long in the pan. Next time, let it cool in the pan for no more than 5 minutes, then transfer it to a wire rack.

The cake collapsed when I cut it into layers. The cake was warm when you cut it. Make sure it has cooled completely, since the cake is fragile when it is warm.

The cream has started to run off the sides of the cake. Your cake was not completely cool when you added the cream.

On cutting the cake the gâteau collapsed and the cream started to ooze out. You may have used too much force when cutting the cake. Next time, use a gentle sawing motion when cutting the cake into slices so you don't squash the layers together.

Try more Gâteau-style Cake recipes ▶ ▶ ▶

Génoise with Raspberries and Cream

**Serves
8–10**

**Bakes in
25–30
minutes**

**4 weeks
unfilled**

Ingredients

3 tbsp unsalted butter, melted, plus
extra for greasing

4 large eggs

½ cup sugar

1 cup all-purpose flour

1 tsp pure vanilla extract

finely grated zest of 1 lemon

2 cups heavy cream

11oz raspberries, plus extra to decorate

1 tbsp confectioners' sugar, plus extra for dusting

Special Equipment

8in (20cm) round springform cake pan

Preheat the oven to 350°F (180°C). Grease the cake
pan and line the bottom with parchment paper.

BEAT THE MIXTURE

Bring a saucepan of water to just below
a boil, then remove from the heat. Sit a large
heatproof bowl over the pan, making sure that the
bottom of the bowl doesn't touch the water. Add
the eggs and sugar to the bowl and, using a hand
mixer, beat for 5 minutes or until very thick
and the beaters leave a trail when lifted. The
mixture will increase up to 5 times its original
volume. Remove from the heat, beat for 1 minute
more, and cool.

Sift the flour into the bowl and carefully fold
it in with the vanilla, lemon zest, and melted
butter, taking care you don't knock any air out
of the mixture.

BAKE THE CAKE

Spoon the mixture into the pan and bake for
25–30 minutes, or until the top is springy and
golden brown. Test with a metal skewer and if it
comes out clean from the center of the cake, it is
done, and if not, simply bake for few minutes more
and test again. Let the cake cool in its pan for
4–5 minutes, since it is very fragile at this stage.
Then turn the cake onto a wire rack, removing the
parchment paper, and let it cool completely.

Tip Run a knife around the edge of the pan before
removing the cake to ensure clean sides.

FILL AND SERVE

Whip the heavy cream in a large bowl until
it forms soft peaks. Lightly crush 11oz (325g) of the
raspberries with the confectioners' sugar and fold
into the cream, leaving behind any raspberry juice
so as not to make the cream too wet.

Carefully cut the cooled cake into 3 equal
horizontal layers using a serrated knife. Place
the bottom layer on a serving plate and spread
with half of the cream mixture. Top with the
second layer and spread with the remaining
cream. Top the cake with the final layer, then
decorate with the remaining raspberries. Dust
with confectioners' sugar before serving in slices.

Chocolate Amaretti Roulade

**Serves
6–8**

**Bakes in
20 minutes**

**8 weeks,
unfilled**

Ingredients

6 large eggs, separated

⅓ cup sugar

½ cup cocoa powder, plus extra for dusting

confectioners' sugar, for dusting

1¼ cups heavy cream

2–3 tbsp Amaretto or brandy

20 Amaretti cookies, crushed, plus 2 for the topping

2oz (50g) dark chocolate, grated

Special Equipment

8 x 11in (20 x 28cm) jelly roll pan

Preheat the oven to 350°F (180°C). Line the base and sides of the pan or baking sheet with parchment paper.

BEAT THE MIXTURE

Bring a saucepan of water to just below a boil, then remove from the heat. Sit a heatproof bowl over the pan, making sure the bottom of the bowl doesn't touch the water. Add the egg yolks and sugar to the bowl and, using a hand mixer, beat for 10 minutes or until thick and creamy. Remove from the heat.

Beat the egg whites in a separate clean bowl with a hand mixer until soft peaks form. Sift the cocoa powder into the yolk mixture, then gently fold in with the beaten egg whites.

Careful! Beat the egg whites in a clean, grease-free bowl, otherwise they won't increase in volume.

BAKE THE CAKE

Pour the mixture into the pan, smoothing it into the corners. Bake in the preheated oven for 20 minutes, or until just firm to the touch and a metal skewer comes out clean. Let cool in its pan for at least 5 minutes before turning, face down, on to parchment paper that has been dusted well with confectioners' sugar. Cool for at least 30 minutes.

Careful! The cake must be completely cool before filling, otherwise the cream will melt.

ASSEMBLE THE CAKE

Whip the heavy cream with a hand mixer until it forms soft peaks. Trim the sides of the cake to neaten them, then drizzle over the Amaretto. Spread the cream over the cake and scatter with the crushed Amaretti cookies. Roll it lengthwise, using the parchment paper to help keep it tightly rolled. Arrange the cake on a serving plate with the seam underneath. Crumble the remaining Amaretti cookies on top. Sprinkle with grated chocolate, dust with confectioners' sugar and cocoa. Serve in slices.

Tip To roll the roulade, hold the longest edge of the parchment farthest from you and lift it up carefully. Pull it toward you, and over the cake as you roll the cake toward you. The parchment will help to contain the cake and shape it into a neat roll.

How to make **Choux Pastry**

Choux pastry is a very light and airy pastry made with egg that is used for baking profiteroles and éclairs. By beating enough air into the soft, doughy mixture you will guarantee crisp and light pastry that will rise beautifully as it bakes.

Beat the mixture with a wooden spoon until it forms a soft dough ball

Careful! Don't overboil the butter and water, since this will cause the water to evaporate. You need the steam from the water to help the pastry rise.

Shooting in the flour

The traditional technique for beating flour into melted butter and water is called "shooting" the flour, meaning you add it all at once. Sift the flour onto a piece of parchment paper, then pour it all into the pan—the flour cooks instantly and evenly. Then beat the mixture vigorously, but stop when it forms a ball of soft dough that comes away from the sides of the pan.

Add the eggs slowly to ensure a soft dough of pipeable consistency

Beat in the eggs using a vigorous action

Beating in the eggs

Using a wooden spoon, beat the eggs into the mixture a little at a time. Adding the eggs one at a time not only makes it easier to incorporate them into the mix, but with each beating you are also adding more air. The dough should now be soft enough to pipe.

Help! If your piped rounds peak up too much at their tips, simply press down lightly, using a dampened finger.

Make sure the rounds are all the same size to guarantee even baking

Piping the dough

Fit your piping bag with a plain nozzle and fill it with the choux dough. With one hand at the top of your piping bag and one at the bottom, squeeze the dough out from the top into even, walnut-sized rounds. Leave space in between each round for spreading and puffing up.

Profiteroles

Profiteroles are puffed buns made from smooth, pipeable choux dough. Try this classic recipe for light, crispy profiteroles, filled with cream and topped with a delicious chocolate sauce.

erves 4 | Bakes in 22 minutes | 12 weeks, unfilled

gredients

:up all-purpose flour

>sp unsalted butter

rge eggs, beaten

all-purpose flour | **unsalted butter** | **beaten eggs**

r the filling and topping

cups heavy cream

: (200g) good-quality dark chocolate, broken into pieces

osp butter

osp corn syrup

heavy cream | **dark chocolate** | **golden syrup**

pecial equipment

iping bags, fitted with a
½in (1cm) plain nozzle and
a ¼in (5mm) star nozzle

piping bags

**plain nozzle and
star nozzle**

Total time *57 minutes, plus cooling*

Prepare
5 minutes

Make
20 minutes

Bake
22 minutes

Decorate
10 minutes

161

1 Preheat the oven to 425°F (220°C). Line 2 sheets with parchment paper. Sift the flour into a bowl, then over low heat melt the butter and ⅔ cup water in a saucepan. Bring to a boil, remove from heat, and add, or "shoot," the flour all at once.

Remember To "shoot" the flour, transfer to a sheet of parchment after sifting into a bowl, then pour it into the saucepan all at once.

Hold the sieve high to get as much air as possible into the flour

2 Beat the mixture together with a wooden spoon until it is smooth and forms a ball. Then let it cool for about 10 minutes.

Careful! Don't be impatient and add the eggs before the dough has had time to cool or you will start to cook them.

3 Gradually add the eggs, a little at a time, beating well after each addition until the eggs are fully incorporated.

Remember The more you beat the mixture, the more you develop the gluten and the more air you will get into it, helping the dough to puff up.

Add about a quarter of the eggs with each addition, beating well each time

4 Continue to beat the dough until you end up with a very smooth and shiny dough. Use a wooden spoon so you don't cut too much into the mixture, since this would break up the developing gluten and result in the buns not setting or rising well.

Remember The dough should be soft, not too sticky, and of a pipeable consistency.

5 Spoon the dough into a piping bag fitted with the plain nozzle. Pipe small rounds, set far enough apart, onto the sheets. Bake for 20 minutes until risen.

Tip If you prefer your choux buns to have a more natural shape, use spoons to shape the dough.

Careful! Don't be tempted to open the oven too early or the buns will deflate.

Make sure you twist the top of the piping bag around to enclose the dough before piping

Flatten the tops of the dough balls by pressing down with a dampened finger

Use a small, sharp knife to make the slits in the buns

6 Remove from the oven, then make a 1in (2.5cm) slit in the side of each choux bun, allowing the steam to escape. Bake for another 2 minutes until golden brown and firm. Cool on a wire rack.

Why? You must slit the buns and let the steam escape, since steam will make them soggy. Work quickly so they don't cool too much.

7 Place ½ cup of the cream in a saucepan, add the chocolate, butter, and syrup, and heat over low heat until melted and smooth. Stir frequently to speed up the melting process.

Why? Heating the ingredients for the sauce over gentle heat prevents the sauce from overheating and separating, also known as "splitting."

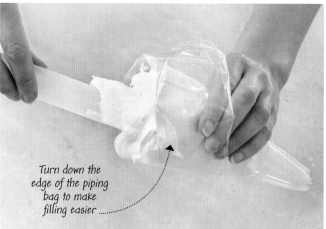

Turn down the edge of the piping bag to make filling easier ....

8 Whip the remainder of the cream until it forms soft peaks. The cream is ready if it holds its shape when the beaters are removed. Spoon the cream into the piping bag with the star nozzle, then twist the top of the bag around to enclose the cream.

Tip To support the bag and make it easier to fill, you can place it in a tall glass (see p.52).

9 With one hand at the top of the bag and the other holding a choux bun, squeeze the cream through the nozzle and into the center of the buns, making sure you don't overfill the buns. Arrange the filled buns into a neat mound on a serving plate, then spoon over the chocolate sauce and serve.

Tip Widen the existing slits in the buns with a sharp knife to make filling easier.

The perfect **Profiteroles**

Your finished choux buns should be light, crisp, and airy, and dry
inside and out.

Chocolate sauce
is smooth, rich,
and glossy .....

Softly whipped
cream gives the
perfect contrast to
the crisp, light
choux buns

Choux buns
are light, airy,
and golden ...

Did anything go wrong?

The choux pastry has cracks on the surface.
You may have beaten the dough for too long after
adding the flour, causing the fat to separate, which
leads to cracks on the surface of the baked buns.
Next time, beat the mixture only until it comes
away from the edges of the pan and forms a ball.

The choux buns are flat. You opened the oven
door before the buns had risen fully.

**The insides of the choux buns are soggy and
still a bit doughy.** Next time, remember to slit
the buns with a knife and bake them until the
insides are completely dry.

The cream filling is starting to melt.
You didn't leave the buns to cool completely
before filling.

The chocolate sauce is granular. You may have
melted the ingredients for the chocolate sauce
over too high a heat, which can cause the
ingredients to separate rather than amalgamate.
Next time, melt them together gently.

**The cream filling has started to run out of
the profiteroles.** The profiteroles may not have
cooled enough before filling or the cream wasn't
whipped enough. Next time, let them cool
completely before filling and also whip the cream
until it forms soft peaks and holds its shape.

Try more Choux Pastry recipes ▶ ▶ ▶

Chocolate Orange Profiteroles

Serves 6 | **Bakes in 22 minutes** | **12 weeks, unfilled**

Ingredients

¾ cups all-purpose flour

4 tbsp unsalted butter

2 large eggs, beaten

2 cups heavy cream

finely grated zest of 1 large orange

3 tbsp Grand Marnier

6oz (150g) good-quality dark chocolate,
  broken into pieces

1¼ cups half-and-half

2 tbsp corn syrup

Special Equipment

2 piping bags fitted with a ½in (1cm) plain
  nozzle and a ¼in (5mm) star nozzle

Preheat the oven to 425°F (220°C). Line
2 large baking sheets with parchment paper.

MAKE THE CHOUX PASTE

Sift the flour onto a sheet of parchment paper
or greaseproof paper.

Remember Lift the sieve high when sifting the
flour to get as much air into it as possible.

Melt the butter with ⅔ cup water in a
saucepan over gentle heat. Bring to a boil,
remove from the heat, and immediately add the
flour. Beat with a wooden spoon until smooth
and the mixture forms a ball. Cool for 10 minutes.
Slowly add the eggs to the pan, a little at a time,
beating well after each addition until you have a
stiff, smooth paste.

SHAPE AND BAKE THE PASTRY

Spoon the mixture into the piping bag fitted
with the ½in (1cm) plain nozzle. Pipe walnut-sized
rounds on the sheets, leaving enough space in
between each bun. Bake in the oven for 20
minutes, or until well risen and golden brown.
Remove from the oven and slit the side of each bun
carefully with a knife to prevent it from getting
soggy. Return to the oven for 2 minutes to crisp up,
then cool completely on a wire rack.

FILL AND DECORATE

To make the filling, beat the heavy cream,
orange zest, and 2 tablespoons of Grand Marnier
together in a bowl using a hand mixer until just
thicker than soft peaks. Spoon the cream into the
other piping bag fitted with the ¼in (5mm) star
nozzle and fill each profiterole with the cream.
To make the chocolate sauce, melt the chocolate,
half-and-half, syrup, and the remaining Grand
Marnier together in a saucepan until smooth.
Arrange the filled profiteroles on a serving plate,
spoon the sauce over, and serve.

Tip The unfilled choux buns will keep well for
up to 2 days if stored in an airtight container.

Chocolate Éclairs

Makes 30

Bakes in 25–30 minutes

12 weeks, unfilled

Ingredients

1 cup all-purpose flour

5 tbsp unsalted butter

3 large eggs, beaten

2 cups heavy cream

5oz (150g) good-quality dark chocolate, broken into pieces

Special Equipment

2 piping bags fitted with a ½in (1cm) plain nozzle

Preheat the oven to 400°F (200°C). Line 2 large baking sheets with parchment paper.

MAKE THE CHOUX PASTE

Sift the flour onto a sheet of parchment paper or greaseproof paper.

Remember Lift the sieve high when sifting the flour to get as much air into it as possible.

Melt the butter with ¾ cup water in a saucepan over gentle heat. Bring to a boil, remove from the heat, and immediately add the flour to the pan. Beat with a wooden spoon until smooth and the mixture forms a ball. Cool for 10 minutes. Slowly add the eggs to the pan, a little at a time, beating well after each addition until all are mixed to a stiff, smooth paste.

SHAPE AND BAKE THE PASTRY

Spoon the mixture into a piping bag fitted with the ½in (1cm) plain nozzle. Pipe 30 4in (10cm) lengths of the mixture onto the baking sheets, cutting the end of the lengths from the bag with a wet knife.

Why? Using a wet knife to cut the pastry into lengths gives the éclairs a clean finish.

Bake the pastry for 20–25 minutes, or until golden brown. Then remove from the oven and slit the side of each carefully with a knife to allow the steam to escape. Return to the oven for 5 minutes until the insides are dried out. Remove and let cool on a wire rack.

FILL AND DECORATE

Beat the cream in a bowl using a hand mixer until soft peaks form. Spoon the cream into the other piping bag, or reuse the first one, ensuring it is washed and dried first. Then pipe the cream into each éclair. Melt the chocolate in a heatproof bowl set over a pan of simmering water until fully melted and smooth. Spoon the chocolate over the tops of the éclairs, allow to set, and then serve.

Remember Do not let the bowl of chocolate come into direct contact with the water, otherwise the chocolate will overheat and become grainy.

Tip The unfilled éclairs will keep well for up to 2 days if stored in an airtight container.

How to make **Danish Pastry**

Danish pastries are made from sweetened, buttery layers of yeast-risen dough. Making the dough is the trickiest part, since you must knead, roll, and fold it a few times, incorporating butter as you go, to create light, flaky layers of pastry. Once you have made the dough, the fun part comes in shaping and filling the different types of pastry—and of course eating them!

Gradually draw in the dry ingredients into the yeast mix to make a rough dough

Careful! Make sure you heat the milk only until it's lukewarm, since too much heat can kill the yeast.

Make a well in the center of the dry ingredients and pour in the yeast and milk mix

Adding the yeast mix

Dissolve and proof the yeast before adding it to the dough. Dissolving the yeast in warm milk ensures it's properly distributed throughout the dough. Proofing the yeast confirms it's alive, shown by a layer of foam forming on the surface of the yeast and milk mix.

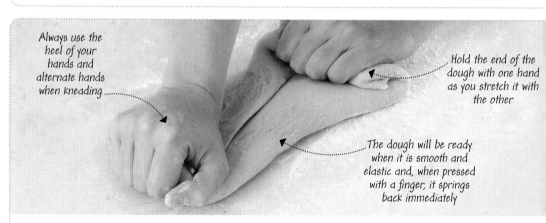

Always use the heel of your hands and alternate hands when kneading

Hold the end of the dough with one hand as you stretch it with the other

The dough will be ready when it is smooth and elastic and, when pressed with a finger, it springs back immediately

Kneading the dough

To develop the protein gluten present in the flour, which helps the dough to rise, knead the dough thoroughly for up to 15 minutes. Press the heel of your hands into the dough, then push it forward away from you. Fold the dough back on itself after stretching, then turn it a quarter-turn after every two kneads. Repeat this process for 15 minutes.

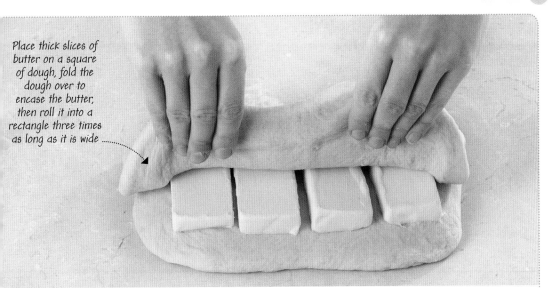

Place thick slices of butter on a square of dough, fold the dough over to encase the butter, then roll it into a rectangle three times as long as it is wide ....

Folding the butter in

The flaky texture of Danish pastry, which is sometimes called "laminated dough," is created by folding butter into the dough.

Distribute the butter evenly through the dough in layers, but make sure it does not melt, since this will make the dough very greasy.

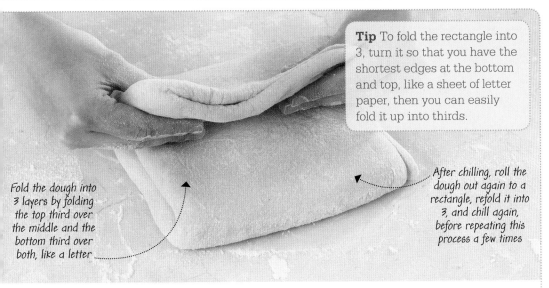

> **Tip** To fold the rectangle into 3, turn it so that you have the shortest edges at the bottom and top, like a sheet of letter paper, then you can easily fold it up into thirds.

Fold the dough into 3 layers by folding the top third over the middle and the bottom third over both, like a letter ....

After chilling, roll the dough out again to a rectangle, refold it into 3, and chill again, before repeating this process a few times

Folding and re-rolling

After folding the rectangle of dough into 3, it's important to chill the dough, since this relaxes it, prevents it from shrinking, and

also stops the butter from seeping out. Always remember to roll the pastry in one direction, since this will distribute the butter evenly.

Danish Pastry

These Danish pastries are deliciously flaky and buttery,
and filled with a sweet jam or compote. Prepare the dough
the night before and keep it in the fridge ready to
roll and bake for a special occasion.

kes 18   **Bakes in**   **Up to 4**
             15–20   **weeks**
             minutes

gredients

:up milk

sp dried yeast

osp sugar

rge eggs, beaten, plus 1 for glazing

cups all-purpose flour, sifted, plus
xtra for dusting

sp salt

getable oil for greasing

tbsp chilled butter

:up good-quality apricot, cherry,
or strawberry jam or compote

milk

dried yeast

beaten eggs

sugar

all-purpose flour

salt

vegetable oil

chilled butter

apricot jam

Total time *2 hours 20–25 minutes, including chilling and rising time*

Prepare
5 minutes

Make *30 minutes + 1 hour
chilling and 30 minutes rising*

Bake
15–20 minutes

1 Heat the milk very gently in a saucepan until lukewarm and no hotter, since too much heat can kill the yeast. Mix the warmed milk, yeast, and 1 tablespoon of the sugar together, cover, and leave for 20 minutes, until frothy. Then beat the eggs into the yeast mixture. In a separate bowl, sift the flour, salt, and the remaining sugar and make a well in the center. Pour in the yeast and egg mixture.

Your yeast mixture should look slightly bubbly and frothy after standing

Knead the dough by pushing it away from you, then folding it back on itself

2 Using a wooden spoon, mix all the ingredients together until they form a soft dough. Turn the dough out onto a floured surface and knead for 15 minutes. Grease a bowl with the oil, add the dough, cover with plastic wrap. Refrigerate for 15 minutes.

Why? You need to chill the dough to help relax its gluten and so prevent the dough from becoming tough.

3 Roll the rested dough out by gently pushing the rolling pin across the dough's length. Turn it by a quarter-turn every few rolls and continue to roll until you have a square measuring about 10in x 10in (25cm x 25cm). Cut the butter into 4 even slices.

Careful! Ensure the butter slices are an even thickness as this is key to achieving even layers of pastry.

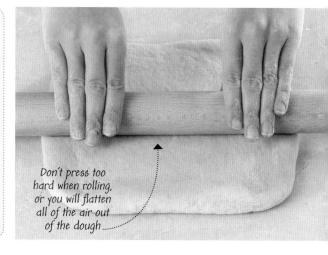

Don't press too hard when rolling, or you will flatten all of the air out of the dough

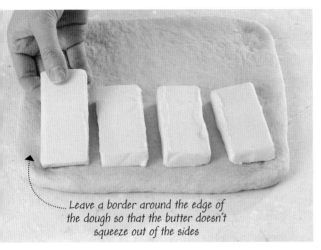

4 Lay the butter slices on one half of the dough, leaving a border of ½–¾in (1–2cm). Fold the other half of the dough over the top, pressing the edges with a rolling pin to seal.

Why? Sealing the edges of the dough contains the butter and prevents it from escaping when you start rolling out the dough.

..... Leave a border around the edge of the dough so that the butter doesn't squeeze out of the sides

5 Flour the dough and roll into a rectangle three times as long as it is wide and ½in (1cm) thick.

Why? You roll the pastry into a rectangle three times longer than it is wide so you can easily fold it into thirds.

Help! If your butter starts to break out of the dough, either at the sides or through the dough itself, simply chill for 15 minutes and try again.

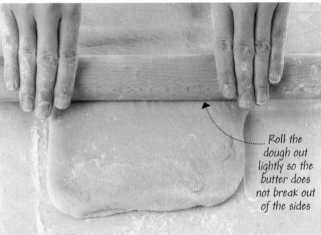

Roll the dough out lightly so the butter does not break out of the sides

Fold the dough into even thirds to create the layers for the pastry

Chill the dough each time you roll and fold it so the butter doesn't get too soft .....

6 Fold the top third down into the middle, then the bottom third back over it, forming a neat rectangle. Wrap the folded dough in plastic wrap and chill for 15 minutes. Roll it out again into a rectangle, as in step 5 and fold again before chilling for another 15 minutes. Then repeat the steps—rolling, folding, and chilling—one more time. Always chill so the butter doesn't get too soft and the gluten relaxes.

7 Cut the dough in half, then roll each half out to a 12in x 12in (30cm x 30cm) square, ¼in (5mm) thick, by gently pushing the rolling pin across the dough and turning a quarter-turn after every few rolls. Cut each square into 9 squares measuring 4in x 4in (10cm x 10cm) to give you a total of 18 squares. Make diagonal cuts from each corner to within ½in (1cm) of the center.

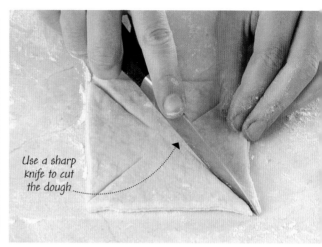

Use a sharp knife to cut the dough

Make sure each corner doesn't overlap

8 Put 1 teaspoon of jam or compote in the center of each square, and fold each corner into the center. The jam or compote in the middle acts as glue to hold the pastry in the center.

Careful! Don't overlap the corners of the pastry or the pastry might not cook through properly.

9 Spoon more jam or compote into the center of each pastry, and place on a baking sheet lined with parchment. Cover with plastic wrap and let rise for 30 minutes to set their shape. Preheat the oven to 400°F (200°C). Brush the pastries with egg wash. Bake for 15–20 minutes until golden brown.

Why? You brush the pastries with egg wash before baking to give them a beautiful glaze.

The perfect **Danish Pastry**

The perfect Danish pastry will be deliciously light and flaky with many layers and a beautifully soft texture.

Perfectly shaped pastries encase a golden pool of jam or compote

Light and flaky layers of buttery pastry

Did anything go wrong?

The Danish pastry is very flat. You may have rolled the dough out too thinly or left it to prove for too long, and the pastry collapsed.

The Danish pastry is far too greasy. Remember to chill the dough during the making, rolling, and folding stages, since insufficient chilling causes the butter to escape.

The Danish pastries have come apart on baking. You may not have left them to rest for the final time to set their shape before baking.

The Danish pastries are tough and hard. You may have overworked the dough and didn't let it rest for long enough.

The Danish pastries are very sticky and the jam has run over the edges. You may have put too much jam or compote in the center, causing it to run over the edges during baking. Next time, add just a teaspoonful to the center once folded.

Try more Danish Pastry recipes ▶ ▶ ▶

Almond Crescents

**Makes
18**

**Bakes in
15–20
minutes**

**Up to
4 weeks**

Ingredients

1 quantity Danish pastry dough (pp.171–73, steps 1–6)

2 tbsp unsalted butter, softened

⅓ cup sugar

¾ cup ground almonds

1 large egg, beaten for glazing

confectioners' sugar, to serve

Line 2 baking sheets with parchment paper.

SHAPE THE DOUGH

Roll half the dough out on a lightly floured surface to a 12in (30cm) square. Trim the edges to neaten, then cut into nine 4in (10cm) squares. Repeat with the remaining dough until you have 18 squares.

Remember Make sure your dough is thoroughly chilled when rolling out and cutting. This way it will hold its shape better.

MAKE THE FILLING AND ASSEMBLE

To make the almond paste, cream together the butter and sugar with an electric mixer, then beat in the ground almonds until smooth. Divide the paste into 18 small balls, and roll each one into a sausage shape a little shorter than the length of the dough squares. Place a roll of the almond paste at one edge of each square, leaving a gap of ¾in (2cm). Press it down and brush the clear edge with egg, then fold the dough over the paste to incorporate it. Press the dough down to seal.

Remember It is important to brush the edges of the pastries with egg to make sure that they are well sealed. This will stop the filling from escaping through the edges of the pastry on baking.

Using a sharp knife, make 4 cuts in the folded edge of each pastry. Transfer to the baking sheets, cover, and let rise for 30 minutes in a warm place. Preheat the oven to 400°F (200°C).

BAKE AND SERVE

Form a crescent shape by bending the edges of the pastries. Brush with egg and bake in the top of the oven for 15–20 minutes, until crisp and golden in color. Cool for 5 minutes on the baking sheet, then transfer to wire racks to cool completely. Dust with confectioners' sugar and serve.

Careful! The baked crescents will be very fragile and should be left to cool down and firm up a little on their baking sheets before moving to wire racks.

Apricot Pastries

Makes 18

Bakes in 15–20 minutes

Unsuitable for freezing

Ingredients

1 quantity Danish pastry dough (pp.171–73, steps 1–6)

½ cup apricot jam

2 x 14oz (400g) cans apricot halves, drained

1 large egg, beaten for glazing

Line 2 baking sheets with parchment paper.

SHAPE THE DOUGH

Roll half the dough out on a lightly floured surface to a 12in (30cm) square. Trim the edges to neaten, then cut into nine 4in (10cm) squares. Repeat with the remaining dough until you have 18 squares.

ASSEMBLE THE PASTRIES

Purée or sieve the apricot jam if it has lumps in it. Take 1 tablespoon of the apricot jam per square and, using the back of a spoon, spread it all over the square leaving a border of about ½in (1cm). Take 2 apricot halves and trim a little off their bottoms if too chunky.

Why? If the apricots are too chunky the pastry won't be able to wrap around and envelop them.

Place the apricot halves in 2 opposite corners of the square. Take the 2 corners without apricots and fold them into the middle to partly cover the apricots. Repeat with the remaining dough and apricots until you have 18 pastries. Arrange on the baking sheets, cover, and let rise for 30 minutes in a warm place. Preheat the oven to 400°F (200°C).

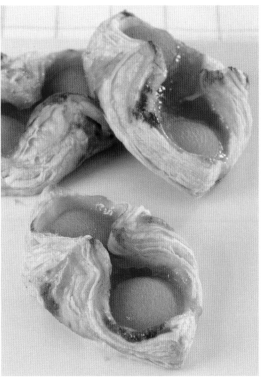

BAKE, GLAZE, AND SERVE

Brush the pastries with egg and bake in the top of the oven for 15–20 minutes until crisp and golden in color. Melt the remaining apricot jam and brush over the pastries to glaze. Cool for 5 minutes on the baking sheet, then transfer to wire racks to cool completely.

Remember Make sure your apricot jam is smooth and lump-free before brushing over the baked pastries.

How to make **Artisan Breads**

Artisan breads are similar to yeast-risen breads, but use a different technique in preparing the yeast, known as "pre-fermentation." This gives the loaf a unique, slightly sour flavor and an interesting texture. A true artisan bread relies on cultivating the yeast naturally present in flour, so the following sourdough recipe is a bit of a "cheat's" version, since domestic yeast has been added. Different methods of pre-fermentation are known as a "starter" or a "sponge," each giving slightly different characteristics to the finished loaves.

The mixture will have increased in volume very slightly after fermenting

Stir the starter with a wooden spoon

As the yeast ferments, stir it once every day to ensure it doesn't end up in a solid mass

Tip To keep the starter active, healthy, and going indefinitely, stir it every 2–3 weeks to knock out the air, and also discard half of it, mixing in a fresh batch of ¾ cup flour and 1 cup water. Do the same each time you use the starter to make a new loaf. Don't store it at a high temperature. Store it in a fridge, but bring back to room temperature before using.

Preparing the starter

Leave the yeast to stand or "ferment" in warm water and a little flour for 24 hours. Both the yeast and the bacteria naturally present during fermentation feed on the sugars in the flour, producing acidic by-products, giving the loaf its characteristic sour flavor. After 24 hours, by which time the mix will be a little frothy, stir the mix and leave to ferment for 2–4 days. The mix will produce more carbon dioxide, and it will look bubbly and develop a pleasant sour smell, vital for a good sourdough bread. The longer you leave it, the stronger the flavor of the bread will be.

Sponge will be well risen and slightly puffy in appearance when ready

More yeast is then added to the risen sponge with the strong white bread flour to form the baguette

Making a baguette sponge

A baguette's soft dough calls for a "sponge" method of pre-fermentation. Dissolve your yeast in warm water and a little flour, and let it rise for 12 hours. By leaving the sponge only for 12 hours, the gluten will not develop quite as much as in a sourdough starter, thus giving the baguette a slightly softer texture. The resulting sponge, which you mix with other ingredients, will also be slightly drier and firmer.

Starter should be bubbly and frothy

Mix until no flecks of flour are visible

Making an overnight starter

For an overnight starter, used in rye bread, mix the yeast with warm water, yogurt, and molasses, and let stand overnight, allowing the yeast to feed off the sugar in the molasses to produce carbon dioxide. It is now ready to be mixed with the other ingredients to make a dough.

Sourdough Loaf

You'll need to plan ahead for this deliciously tangy
sourdough loaf, since the recipe uses both a starter and
a sponge, requiring at least four days of pre-fermentation.
The unique flavor and texture of the loaf, however, will
be well worth the effort and if you keep your starter
going you can bake sourdough every day.

**Makes
loaves**

**Bakes in
40–45
minutes**

**Up to 8
weeks**

gredients

r the sourdough starter

bsp dried yeast

cups bread flour

r the sponge

cups bread flour,
plus 3 tbsp for sprinkling

r the bread

tsp dried yeast

cups bread flour, plus extra for dusting

bsp salt

getable oil, for greasing

lenta or fine yellow cornmeal, for
dusting

andful of ice cubes

pecial Equipment

heets of muslin

dried yeast

salt

bread flour

ice cubes   **polenta**

muslin   **vegetable oil**

Total time *3 hours 5–40 minutes, including 2–2½ hours proofing
time and 4–6 days fermenting time*

 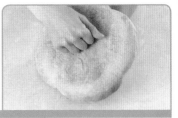

● **Prepare**
4–6 days fermenting

● **Make** *25 minutes
+ 2–2½ hours rising*

● **Bake**
40–45 minutes

1 Make your starter 4–6 days before you want to bake your loaf by dissolving the yeast in a bowl with 2 cups lukewarm water. Stir in the flour, then cover, and leave to ferment in a warm place for 24 hours. Stir again, re-cover, and ferment for another 2–4 days, stirring every day.

Why? You need to stir your starter every day to keep the mixture from becoming a solid mass.

Starter should be frothy and have a sour odor after 24 hours

2 For the sponge, mix 1 cup of the fermented starter with an equal amount of lukewarm water in a bowl.

Why? Measure out only 1 cup of the starter, since it will have created more than this during fermentation.

Careful! Use only lukewarm water or you will kill off the yeast.

Use only 1 cup of the starter

3 Stir in the flour, mix vigorously, and sprinkle with another 3 tablespoons of flour. Cover the sponge with a damp dish towel and let ferment overnight, once again, in a warm place.

Why? A damp dish towel creates the perfect moist environment for the yeast to continue developing.

Dough will
be slightly
sticky at
this stage

4 To make the bread, dissolve
the remaining yeast in
4 tablespoons of lukewarm water
and mix it into the sponge. Stir in
half the flour and salt, and mix
well. Gradually add the remaining
flour and mix to form a soft dough.

Why? Mixing the flour in
2 batches ensures the yeast and
sponge are evenly distributed
within the flour.

5 Knead the dough (see p.132) on
a floured surface for 10
minutes, until very smooth and
elastic. Oil a bowl, place the dough
in it, cover with a damp dish towel,
and let rise for 1–1½ hours in a
warm place, until it doubles in size.

Remember Kneading helps
to create gluten in the dough,
allowing it to stretch as it rises.
Without lengthy kneading your
bread will be heavy and flat.

Dough is
ready if it
springs back
when lightly
pressed with
a finger

Use your fists to
punch the excess
air from the dough
by punching it

6 Turn the dough out again
and punch down the dough
to remove excess air. Cut into
2 equal parts, then shape each
into a rough ball by pulling the
ends into the center underneath
and pressing them together lightly
to form a seam.

Why? Punching down evens
out the texture of the dough
and redistributes the yeast.

7 Place each round of dough into a bowl, each lined with 2 pieces of muslin and lightly dusted with flour. Cover with a dish towel and leave to rise again for 1 hour in a warm place, or until the dough fills the bowls.

Why? The muslin allows the dough to breathe and prevents it from sticking to the bowl. You can also leave the dough in an oiled bowl, covered with a dish towel.

Dough must be doubled in size before it is ready to bake

Peel the muslin off carefully so as not to knock out any air

8 Preheat the oven to 400°F (200°C). Sprinkle 2 baking sheets with polenta, and place a loaf on each sheet, seam side down on top of the polenta. Peel off the muslin.

Why? Dusting your baking sheets with polenta gives a nice, textured base to the loaf and prevents the bread from sticking.

9 Cut a cross on the top of each loaf so the dough relaxes and rises properly. Place a roasting pan in the bottom of the oven and put the ice cubes in it. Place the loaves in the oven, and bake for 20 minutes. Reduce to 375°F (190°C), and bake for another 20–25 minutes, until golden in color.

Why? Ice cubes create plenty of steam in the oven, which helps the loaves develop a good crust.

The perfect **Sourdough Loaf**

The perfect sourdough loaf will be beautifully risen and golden in color, with a chewy texture and a distinctive sour taste.

Crispy outer crust is golden brown in color

Texture of the loaf is light, soft, and aerated

Loaf has a tangy, slightly sour flavor

Did anything go wrong?

The bread dough rose during proving but sank during baking. You may have forgotten to add the salt. During long fermentation, yeast can become very active, causing the dough to overprove, but salt will temper this behavior. Salt also helps to create a stronger gluten network in the dough, improving the loaf's volume and preventing it from sinking.

The dough was too flat. You may have added too much liquid to the dough or you overproved the dough. Next time, let dough rise until doubled in size and no more.

The bread is not crispy enough. You may not have built up enough steam in the oven. A humid environment makes the crust crisp. Next time, make sure you put ice cubes in a roasting pan or add more than you did last time.

The dough rose too fast. You may have been working in a warm environment or used too much starter. Next time, you could leave the dough to rise slowly in a fridge overnight—that way it is easier to monitor.

The bread has a very soft crust. You may not have baked the bread for long enough. Make sure the oven is preheated at the correct temperature, and for an extra crispy crust, you can also spray the top of the bread with water before baking. To test if the loaf is baked to perfection, tap the bottom with your knuckles, and if it sounds hollow it is cooked through.

The flavor of the sourdough is too weak. You may not have left the mix to ferment for long enough. Next time, ferment for slightly longer.

Try more Artisan Bread recipes ▶ ▶ ▶

Artisan Rye Bread

Makes 1 loaf **Bakes in 40–50 minutes** **Up to 4 weeks**

Ingredients

For the starter

1 cup rye flour

⅔ cup plain yogurt

1 tsp dried yeast

1 tbsp molasses

1 tsp caraway seeds, lightly crushed

For the dough

1 cup rye flour

1½ cups bread flour, plus extra for dusting

2 tsp salt

1 egg, beaten, for glazing

1 tsp caraway seeds, to decorate

PREPARE THE STARTER

Begin preparing the starter a day ahead. Mix together all of the starter ingredients in a bowl with 1 cup tepid water. Cover and leave to stand overnight. The next day the mixture should be bubbling.

MAKE THE DOUGH

Mix the flours together with the salt, then stir into the starter. Combine to form a dough, adding a little extra water if needed. Turn the dough onto a lightly floured surface and knead for 10 minutes, or until smooth and elastic. Shape the dough into a ball, place in an oiled bowl, and cover loosely with plastic wrap to stop the dough from drying up. Leave in a warm place for 1 hour, or until doubled in size.

SHAPE THE DOUGH

Lightly knead the dough on a floured surface, then shape it into a football shape. Transfer to a floured baking sheet, re-cover it loosely, and let it rise again in a warm place for 30 minutes. Preheat the oven to 425°F (220°C). Brush the dough with the egg and sprinkle over the remaining caraway seeds. With a sharp knife, make 3 slashes in the top of the loaf along its length: this will help the loaf to rise evenly in the oven.

BAKE AND SERVE

Bake for 20 minutes, then reduce the oven to 400°F (200°C). Bake for another 20–30 minutes or until firm and dark golden in color. The bottom of the bread should sound hollow when tapped. Transfer to a wire rack to cool.

Hazelnut and Raisin variation Don't use the caraway seeds. After the initial kneading, shape the dough into a rough rectangle, scatter ½ cup of toasted and coarsely chopped hazelnuts and ¼ cup raisins on top of the dough. Fold the dough over and knead gently until the nuts and raisins are incorporated. Then shape and continue as in recipe.

Whole-wheat Baguette

Makes 2 baguettes **Bakes in 20–25 minutes** **Up to 4 weeks**

Ingredients

½ tsp dried yeast, plus a large pinch for the sponge

1 tbsp rye flour

¾ cup whole-wheat bread flour

vegetable oil for greasing

1¼ cups bread flour,
   plus extra for dusting

½ tsp salt

MAKE THE SPONGE

Prepare the sponge a day ahead. Dissolve a generous pinch of yeast in ¾ cup tepid water. Add the rye flour and ¾ cup of the whole-wheat flour. Form a sticky, loose dough and place in a lightly oiled bowl. Cover with plastic wrap and let stand for at least 12 hours, or overnight.

MAKE THE DOUGH

Dissolve the remaining yeast in 1¼ cup tepid water. Put the risen sponge, the remaining whole-wheat flour, the white flour, and salt into a large bowl. Pour in the dissolved yeast, and stir to form a dough. Knead the dough on a lightly floured surface until smooth and elastic. Put the dough in a lightly oiled bowl, cover with plastic wrap, and leave for 1½–2 hours.

SHAPE THE DOUGH

Turn the dough out onto the floured surface and punch it down. Divide into 2 equal pieces. Knead and shape each into a rough rectangle, then fold both of the long sides into the center and shape into a rounded oblong shape, pinching the edges together in the center to seal. Then turn the dough over so the seam is underneath. Stretch and roll it into a thin, log shape, no more than 1½in (4cm) wide. Place on a floured baking sheet. Cover with

oiled plastic wrap and a dish towel, and let prove until almost doubled in size. Preheat the oven to 450°F (230°C).

BAKE THE DOUGH

The dough is ready to bake when it is tight, well risen, and springs back on touch. Slash it diagonally all along the top using a knife. This will allow for the bread to rise in the oven. Dust the tops with flour, spray with water, and bake in the middle of the oven for 20–25 minutes. The bread will be ready when it is firm and the bottom sounds hollow when tapped. Remove from the oven and cool on wire racks.

White Baguette variation Make the sponge with strong white bread flour. Use 1 teaspoon dried yeast with ⅓ cup white bread flour for the dough.

Index

Acknowledgments

Photographic Credits

Dorling Kindersley would like to thank Dave King
and Peter Anderson for new photography.
All images © Dorling Kindersley
For further information see:
www.dkimages.com

Publisher's Acknowledgments

Dorling Kindersley would like to thank:

In the UK

Design assistance Jessica Bentall, Vicky Read
Editorial assistance Helen Fewster, Holly Kyte
DK Images Claire Bowers, Freddie Marriage, Emma Shepherd,
Romaine Werblow
Indexer Chris Bernstein

In India

Assistant Art Editor Karan Chaudhary
Art Editor Devan Das
Design assistance Ranjita Bhattacharji, Simran Kaur,
Anchal Kaushal, Prashant Kumar, Tanya Mehrotra,
Ankita Mukherjee, Anamica Roy
Editors Kokila Manchanda, Arani Sinha
DTP Designers Rajesh Singh Adhikari, Sourabh Chhallaria,
Arjinder Singh
CTS/DTP Manager Sunil Sharma